PRESSING MATTERS

PRESSING MATTERS

The debates, controversies,
and mysteries that have shaped
the world of wine

Alan Ramey

ACADEMIE DU VIN LIBRARY

Published in 2026 by Académie du Vin Library Ltd
academieduvinlibrary.com

Copyright © Alan Ramey, 2026

The right of Alan Ramey to be identified as the author of this book has been asserted in accordance with the Copyright, Designs and Patents Act 1988.

All rights reserved. No part of this publication may be reproduced, stored in a retrieval system, distributed or transmitted in any form or by any means, including photocopying, recording or other electronic or mechanical methods, and including training for generative artificial intelligence (AI), without the prior written permission of the publisher. Translation into any other language, and subsequent distribution as above, is also expressly forbidden, without prior written permission of the author and publisher.

A CIP catalogue record for this book is available from the British Library
ISBN 978-1-913141-92-9

Brand and product names are trademarks or registered trademarks of their respective owners.

Publisher: Hermione Ireland
Editor: Rebecca Clare
Front cover: James Pople Design
Indexer: Marian Aird

Printed in Great Britain

Contents

A first sip — 1

1. Terroir – the epistemology of taste — 6
2. Rules of wine regions – the liquid codification of geography — 26
3. The organic question — 48
4. Biodynamics: truth or magic? — 77
5. Climate and wine – holding on — 97
6. Aesthetic theories of quality: what can we really taste? — 116
7. The value of wine — 136
8. Naturalness in wine: on the spectrum of industry and purity — 155

A mental digestif — 183

Notes — 186

Index — 209

A first sip

Growing up in a winery, there was one rule my sister and I had to follow if we had an idea about improving wine quality. There had to be an experiment. The experiment could only have one variable, meaning that if we were interested in changing the number of whole cluster bunches added to the fermenter, the composition of the blend, or the temperature of the maceration, we had to pick one. It was vital to have a control trial so that we could confidently compare the change to the original.

This lesson was so deeply ingrained in me that as I entered the broader wine world I assumed every winery operated this way. Surely the only way to make wine was to invest everything in the product itself, relying on objective standards to achieve improvement.

What I saw was something entirely different. Many wineries changed their entire farming or winemaking ideas overnight, and not only that, but proclaimed publicly that they now had all the right answers. They might make claims about the effect of the soil, climate, or some other environmental factor on their wine, but there didn't seem to be much evidence behind the assertions.

Many of these wineries seemed to be rewarded for their audacity. People making claims that their wines were the best or that their regions were the greatest seemed to abound, and a great number of consumers seemed to be drinking it in without skepticism, sometimes paying shockingly large sums of money to do so. Collectors showed off cellars of expensive wines whose value was based on dubious claims.

Studies show that over 50 percent of people believe their driving is better than average, an impossible claim, to be sure. Among wineries, it seemed as if well above 50 percent believed they were in a special place, using a special technique or making a special wine. It didn't add up. The culture wasn't as intellectually rigorous as I had expected. It was not mathematically possible that all the wineries were as great as they said they were.

As I grew up in wine, I was able to ask questions of world experts, blazing minds, and experimental practitioners. I was brought along to winemaking groups and conferences. At the age of 14, I was included in a cellar tasting at Domaine de la Romanée-Conti, one of the most celebrated wineries in the world. I politely turned down all the glasses presented to me. I wasn't even aware that I was in the presence of something special.

As a result of this upbringing, I also became deeply interested in debate. In high school I was on a team of two that made it to the top ten in California; in college, I was half of the number one ranked novice team in the East Coast league. I eventually stopped competing, but I brought an approach of intellectual discourse back to the winery after graduating.

Perhaps it was this background that would lead me to get frustrated in the world of wine. I had received an enviable practical training, worked under amazing mentors in Casablanca and Burgundy, competed on the blind tasting team in graduate school, took chemistry courses after work, read everything I could get my hands on, and continued to pursue the idea that there were correct answers to the big questions in wine. Not everything was subjective, my instincts told me. For a technical product like wine, surely it was possible to find good answers, or at the very least, correctly ascertain what was subjective.

But I continued to see a wine world characterized more by lifestyle and fun than rigor. What troubled me most was that despite the very scientific training of most winemakers and viticulturists, I was witnessing many discourses more tethered to whimsy than to reason.

I began to notice something else too, a schism between the overly scientific and the philosophically-minded pioneers whose visions helped mold the famous wine regions we know today. Some of the most passionate people in the wine business were making points about why certain places and practices held intangible significance, and my rational tools seemed ill equipped to respond to these often ephemeral ideas that seemed to animate the elements of wine that people connected with most strongly.

There seemed to be a disconnect between discourse and practice.

Certain topics were especially puzzling. What made people disagree so vociferously over farming ideologies like organics and biodynamics? Which philosophies animate the natural wine debate, and can natural be defined, for wine or any other product? Why was it that some wines sold for so much money – where did that value come from? How did legal scholars come to codify regional wine rules in so many fascinating ways around the world, and how much of an obstacle did climate change pose to that wine world order? How could you sit down and define what a good glass of wine was, anyway? And, to channel Jerry Seinfeld, What's the deal with terroir?

These questions kept returning to me. I couldn't understand how incredibly intelligent people came to such different conclusions on these foundational matters. What made these topics so insurmountable? I became obsessed with trying to understand these hard questions of wine, and the more I researched the more I began to notice a pattern.

Firstly, these hard questions involved more than learning mere facts. A trove of wine trivia cards would only go so far. These were past the surface level and into the hows and whys of wine. And secondly, these hard questions were multidisciplinary. They couldn't be answered by microbiologists, psychologists, sensory scientists, anthropologists, or philosophers in isolation. It was only possible to begin looking for answers by approaching authorities in several disciplines, groping toward a distant light at the end of a very long tunnel.

Not only did this approach offer counterintuitive insight, but it was more fun, too. To answer these questions, I reviewed academic journals, countless books, and contacted over a hundred academics and experts from all over the world, with degrees and backgrounds in all different sorts of fields and endeavors. From microbiologists, chemists, and botanists to historians, activists, and even a religious scholar – for me it became ever more clear that the joy of wine is that it is one of those fields that opens up to a million different lenses of investigation and wonder. To look at wine is to look into a mirror back at the world.

This book is about that adventure – looking at the messiest and most contested issues in wine, and in so doing, seeing wine through a new lens. Rather than beginning with what we know, by approaching it from the perspectives that confuse, challenge, or fill us with wonder, we are perhaps gaining a valuable way to see the world and ourselves.

In much the same way that the best sports movies can be enjoyed both by those who love the sport and those who know little about it, I hope this book appeals to established wine appreciators wishing to expand their knowledge and to newcomers interested in understanding wine's place in the bigger picture and in what wine has to say about the human condition.

Because each multifaceted topic is covered in just one chapter, I don't pretend to resolve the discussion or to cite every relevant source. This would not be possible or advisable for a book of this short size.

Nor do I intend to impose my own personal views to neatly wrap up each issue. The chapters will not end in satisfying realizations of a singular truth. The satisfaction, I hope, will come from engaging with a broader spectrum of discourse on each topic and reaching a deeper understanding. Each issue opens up further questions for pondering, and I don't want to disrespect the sanctity of open and free thought with my very mortal and no-doubt flawed opinions.

I have, to the best of my abilities, limited my biases. My goal instead has been to showcase an introduction to each discourse by getting to know some of the most educated and passionate people working on these issues. I hope that by hearing the different perspectives on these issues you can make up your own mind. If this book propels you to further investigate from a place of curiosity, that would make me happy.

Perhaps having read this book, the next time you look at a glass of wine and take a sip you will be able to appreciate it not solely for its flavor, but for the entire history of intellectual thought that goes into it.

Cheers, nerds – onwards and forwards. Here's to curiosity.

1
Terroir – the epistemology of taste

"Without a sense of place the work is often reduced to a cry of voices in empty rooms, a literature of the self, at its best poetic music; at its worst a thin gruel of the ego."

William Kennedy

"If you don't know where you are, you don't know who you are."

Wendell Berry

"At its most extreme, we might argue that the EU has sought to enlist the power and imaginary of regions and terroir in much the same way as the nineteenth century 'nation builders' used these same building blocks as part of a process of construction of, for example, a French, Belgian, German or Polish nationhood." [1]

Marion Demossier

To listen to members of the wine trade talk about terroir, you'd be forgiven for assuming they were discussing religion. Jean Anthelme Brillat-Savarin, in his much-venerated 1826 opus, *The Physiology of Taste*, opines that the capacity to determine the provenance of taste is a "point of perfection."[2] This recognition of typicity, the somewhereness of a wine, is for many the sensorial proof that winemaking regions matter – it is the vindication of wine as a form of expressing nature.

That the place a wine is from leaves a trace – a proverbial footprint – has led to a community and a culture of gustatory sleuths who derive their drinking pleasure not from tipsiness but from uncovering olfactory clues. Through studying the taste profile, alcohol, acid level, and myriad other factors, curious tipplers can transform any glass of wine into a game of chess for the nose and taste buds.

The first record of the word terroir dates from the seventeenth century. A French dictionary defines the term as "earth considered with respect to agriculture."[3] This delightfully poetic clarification was a distillation of knowledge that had arguably been understood for centuries. A primordial ancestor of the modern concept of terroir was conceivably in effect in the Middle Ages, where viticultural neighborhoods were appreciated for their different quality levels.[4] By carbon-dating ancient vessels, archeologists have estimated that winemaking at a reasonable scale existed at least some 7,000 years ago, around 5400 BC, with records showing that in Ancient Egypt, Greece, and Rome there were preferred wine growing regions. Inasmuch as these regions were preferred for quality, it may have been that humans in these ancient civilizations developed some notion of site-specific quality evaluation, an inkling of terroir. The exact historical origin, when humans first began to think this way, is a mystery.

The connotation of the word terroir has shifted significantly since it was first used. Originally, the earthy or dirty nature of the word had a negative connotation, for example a person "smelling of terroir" indicated someone with flaws, or somebody speaking with a terroir accent implied that they spoke with a country accent.[5] The word's metamorphosis to a positive concept didn't occur until the 1950s, 1960s and onwards.[6]

The demarcation of the Douro in 1756 was the first lawfully significant move to codify the terroir ideal[7] but it was not until France created the Appellation d'Origine Controlée (AOC) in 1935 that the modern incarnation of state-sanctioned terroir as we know it today was set in stone. Enshrined in these laws were not only the physical boundaries from region to region, but the rules under which these growers had to operate to place the regional designation on their bottle. Countries around the world followed, with varying degrees of legal strictures.

In Italy's Denominazione di Origine Controllata e Garantita (DOCG) system, the government determines the grape variety and harvest yield, amongst other rules, and the wine must pass a tasting test to ensure it is deemed representative of that region's historic style. Chile and the United States, by comparison, have delimited wine regions, but not the same strictness for rules of production. These different standards elucidate the difficulty in finding a unanimous definition of terroir and foreshadow the debates that have emerged.

* * *

Of the foundational mysteries, uncertainties, and disagreements about terroir, the first question to ask is: What constitutes it? What natural elements in and around a vineyard are most causal in creating a distinctive wine and which of these make a place better or worse for wine grapes? The fact that the word terroir derives from *terre*, the French word for earth, is not a linguistic accident, and this is the first aspect of nature surrounding a vineyard that has been given importance in how a wine tastes. "For centuries, for millennia, people thought that vines grew by eating the soil, and wine was God's gift to us from the vine that was made of soil," says Dr. Alex Maltman, a British geologist.[8]

Maltman, who received his PhD from the University of Illinois, has spent his career researching and teaching geology at Aberystwyth University along the coast of Wales. He became critical of the way the word terroir was used by the wine trade. "About twenty, thirty years ago, for some people, the word was hijacked and suddenly reduced down to just being the soil," he muses. The irony that Maltman comes from a geological background but has spent a good portion of his life dispelling the importance of his field within the context of wine is not lost on him.

In Maltman's reading, popular wine writing, and even the informational material presented by wineries, overinflates soil at the expense of climate, leading to the impression that soil has a direct effect on wine's flavor profile. "I see all the time in popular magazines people saying I'm getting minerality because of the soil. They might not be explicitly saying minerals have been transmitted through, but they're implicitly saying the minerality is there because of the soil. So I don't think the battle is completely won."[9] The minerals in soil that many claim wine tastes like do not have a taste and are not soluble in water, so the idea that they are moving from the roots, through the xylem and into the grapes does not seem scientifically plausible.

Though there have certainly been those without geology degrees making scientifically unsound statements about how plants assimilate minerals, there are others who defend soil poetry in wine writing so long as it's grounded in facts. To state that wine smells strikingly like the soil that its vines grow in, and to wax eloquent, is not necessarily a crime against science. They might say that it is fair to marvel at the ability of wine to taste like elements of the natural world from which it comes. In fact, it's this very feature of grapes, that they have so many aromatic esters that can change due to environmental influences that makes wine so much more compelling than carrot juice or a spinach smoothie.

Another geologist pulled into this debate is Françoise Vannier. With a career in the oil and gas sector, she almost ended up working in Angola, but various circumstances landed her in Dijon instead. Assessing the level of knowledge of soil science as it relates to terroir, Vannier became skeptical of the vignerons' knowledge, stating, "Very rapidly, I realized that the wine growers talked a lot about their terroirs – limestone, clay – but they knew nothing regarding that,"[10] explaining her reaction to many vintners in Burgundy throughout her two-decade career studying and mapping soils in the region. She describes the stories often told about soils as "fairy tales."

One of her first jobs was for the wine growers of Meursault, where she was tasked with mapping the soil and subsoil to see if there was a relationship to the taste profiles of vineyards and the hierarchy of soil sites. "I tried to associate wine tasting notes with types of rocks. I was convinced there was a direct relationship," she reflected, but her research didn't back this longstanding idea up. "Nothing was clear," she added. What might have been a bland scientific conclusion elsewhere had the potential for shockwaves in Burgundy, a place where the connection of wine and soil is sacrosanct.

Backing up this skepticism over soil's direct imprint on wine, a review paper by Cornelis (Kees) van Leeuwen and Gerard Seguin observe that the most respected producers in Bordeaux come from a range of different soils, from the limestone at Ausone and the acidic gravel at Lafite Rothschild to the heavy clay at Petrus and Cheval Blanc. "It is generally not possible to equate a soil map of a given region with a map of quality potential for wine-growing,"[11] they note. At UC Davis in California, Albert Julius Winkler, a prominent academic who chaired the department of viticulture from 1935 to 1957, wrote in the *General Viticulture* textbook that "the differences in the character of wines can hardly be attributed to specific soil types."[12] This sort of evidence begins to build a pessimistic picture for those subscribing to the belief that each soil has a distinctive taste.

Although some individuals certainly suppose that large or complex minerals from the earth are transported through the xylem of the vine into the grape, creating a direct link to soil, scientists dismiss this, though many would argue that the link doesn't have to be direct to be legitimate. When Chablis is described as chalky, and chalkiness is noted on the wine, it's possible to acknowledge the coincidental nature of this while also pointing to other soil-based factors that change the way the wine tastes.

Several academics, skeptical of the way that soil has been presented, acknowledge its importance in vine-growing. One of the main phenomena thought to influence the taste of wine is water's interaction with soil type and structure. Vannier observes, "In my opinion, the most important thing is the hydric stress –

the hydric regime – how much water is available for the plants and when."[13] It's theorized that soils that are kept constantly hydrated can lead to watery tasting wines. Though this might be a negative instance, it is suggested to be an example of terroir in action.

One type of soil that retains water is clay. Regardless of the type of clay, with its platelike structure and smaller particulate size compared to silt or sand, pound for pound it can retain more water. Apart from soil type, topography and topsoil depth can significantly affect the water holding capacity of a plot of land, which can have a major effect on the finished wine.

There are several other soil properties affecting how vines grow that are theorized to impact the taste of a finished wine, not all of which will be addressed here. One of the key elements is nitrogen in the soil, which can affect yeast assimilable nitrogen (YAN) in the harvested grapes. (YAN is a measure of the nitrogen that is available to yeast in fermentation, so is a very important metric for winemakers to keep track of.) Too little nitrogen, and the fermentation might fail.[14] However, if nitrogen is too high, there is some research showing that it can inhibit quality in red wines.[15] The fact that farmers affect nitrogen and other nutritional elements through soil fertilization complicates the question of whether the level of nitrogen in the soil should be viewed as an element of the soil or human factor.

Apart from soil, the next biggest environmental factor in the terroir equation is climate. Assuming that all other winemaking approaches are held constant, does a Shiraz from Barossa taste different from a Syrah from Côte-Rôtie more because of the climate or the soil? Which factor is more significant in creating the sense of typicity of each wine? This question has practical implications for future vineyard plantings. On the west coast of the United States, some vintners sought out limestone, such as Josh Jensen, while others sought out cool climates, for example in San Luis Obispo, Sonoma or Mendocino Coast, and Willamette. Many of the vineyards of southern Britain are on Kimmeridgian limestone, which is also commonly found in Champagne.

As Britain develops its wine scene, many are focusing on this similarity in the belief that it is important for sparkling wine. But would these growers do better to forgo the Kimmeridgian rush and instead seek out the warmest places that can ripen grapes in this still extremely marginal climate? Which approach would bear more and better fruit?

Greg Jones is one of the most qualified people in the world to pick apart these questions. Armed with a PhD in environmental science focusing on atmospheric sciences, Jones was a prolific wine climate researcher before returning to his family's winery in the Umpqua Valley of the Pacific Northwest. "Climate is the baseline, period," he says. "I see that if you don't get the climate right, it doesn't matter what the soil is."[16]

Vines grown in a hot climate will likely produce a wine with riper fruit, which usually means higher sugars, and therefore higher alcohol. In extreme cases if the fruit becomes raisinated on the vine, those flavors might shine through in the glass for years or even decades later. By contrast, vines grown in a cool climate might engender lower alcohols, and in extreme cases, underripe flavors coming from compounds called pyrazines. Given the power of climate, one could argue that the effect of soil is overstated and that regional style is born more from the air than *terre*.

In the 1940s, Albert Winkler, the UC Davis professor who went on to dismiss soil as unimportant to wine character, collaborated with a colleague, Maynard Amerine, to split up California into regions based on their temperature summation (a measure of accumulated heat) to help determine which grapes could be grown where. The template was intended as a guide to help wine growers select the right varieties for their sites. The fact that soil type was excluded from this determination process was telling.

Advancing on this somewhat, Jones created a chart showing the range of mean average growing season temperatures, overlaying which varieties were predominantly grown in which climate. It became clear that certain varieties such as Pinot Noir had a narrow range of temperature, precluding them from warmer areas. There was not a similar limitation for soil types. The implication is that within the complex interaction between climate and soil, climate is the more important factor.

The challenge of untangling the roles of two such foundational elements of terroir calls for increasing levels of nuance. Adding in topography helps illustrate the difficulty of uncoupling soil and climate. As a slope's aspect and elevation change, it impacts soil drainage while also altering the site's temperature relative to even adjacent hillsides. Isolating and ranking each element's influence is profoundly difficult. It is unnecessary to list all facets of site identity impacting fruit quality to appreciate that the exercise of teasing apart their import is challenging.

In extreme cases where soils are too toxic for vine establishment or climate is obviously inhospitable (there is no Saharan Chardonnay or Cabernet Franc from the Everglades) the conversation is moot, but among existing wine regions the question matters for drinkers. Whether it's Rhône versus Barossa or Saint-Estèphe versus Calistoga, are these choices all relative, or can it be said that one has better terroir than the other? There is a tendency of some within the world of wine criticism to publicly plead the gustatory equivalent of moral relativism for a question like this, claiming that each country's wines might taste differently but are not qualitatively different. But at the wine bar, preferences show more easily.

Before even getting into taste, another element to consider is whether a particular terroir is environmentally suited to grapevines to begin with. The possibility of making good wine in a place does not equate to the need to do so. If a site produces variable and pitifully low yields (below the standard low yields for quality grapes) and if it requires much more use of pesticides, water or other resources, how is this to be weighed against the resulting taste? Environmentalists might call this a poor site but hedonism-chasing drinkers might view it as the center of the vinous world.

As for wines that show more typicity of place, some academic attempts have been made to find characteristics of climate or soil that more readily lead to this expressiveness. One theory by Pascal Ribéreau-Gayon and Émile Peynaud proposed that more place-expressive wines come from regions where the cultivar is not forced to ripen quickly, and is only harvested in cool enough places to maintain aromas.[17] The question is to what degree of coolness. A 2022 paper entitled "Aromatic maturity is a cornerstone of terroir expression in red wine" stressed the importance of picking within a not-too-ripe and not-underripe window such that these types of aromatic esters could be revealed in the wine, showcasing place.[18]

Although wines from very hot and very cool regions are often frowned upon in terms of quality, there is a counterargument to suggest that a wine showcasing overly ripe or underripe flavors is still expressing its place – it's just not very good. Arguably flavors of underripe pyrazine (think green bell pepper) or overripe notes (think raisins) dominate at the expense of any other subtlety, which would then lead to the argument that they are not exemplars of regional typicity. The complexity and distinction of aromatic compounds within the range of non-extreme viticulture is the ultimate determinant of place-based taste.

In terms of soil, academics agree that sites with good drainage are important. There is a thriving discussion on the costs, benefits, and different attributes of soils, but it is difficult for curious drinkers to figure out which flavors are soil-influenced because it is hard to determine whether winemaking or climate might be playing a role. Most of the research is based on how to avoid the potential excesses of certain soils. For example, for soil conditions leading to excess vine vigor, common practices include, amongst others, selecting a low-vigor rootstock, increasing vine spacing or introducing competition through cover crop establishment. For meager soils, the importance of good nutrition is emphasized.

The implication of this for practical farming leads to the next big topic within terroir – to what degree, if at all, should human intervention be included as part of the definition, and what practices in winemaking and viticulture reveal or conceal the perception of terroir? Common viticultural strategies involve minimizing temperature pressure on vineyards. For example, in a cool climate, a viticulturist might remove leaves to let in sunshine and drop some of the crop so that the remaining clusters ripen before the end of fall. In a warm climate, the vintner might adjust the canopy to shade the vines from the sun. If the wines from these two vineyards and regions taste similar, despite their different climates, it is because they were farmed for what both vintners consider ideal for quality.

It is this sort of difficulty with disentangling the farming from the site that has led some to have a more inclusive definition of terroir that includes human cultivation, particularly when this activity has been a long-standing cultural practice. In a 2012 linguistics paper comparing how different groups use the word terroir, the researchers note, "Due in part to the fact that the word terroir has yet to be properly defined, the various users are likely to communicate differently about the product, leading to incongruent interpretations of terroir."[19] *The Oxford Companion to Wine* summarizes terroir as "the total natural environment of any viticulture site," but continues extensively, acknowledging the difficulty in coming up with a definition and the back and forth about whether human and cultural actions should be part of the definition or not.[20] A more stridently anthropological perspective characterizes the influence of people as not just part of the term, but integral to the entire concept.

Daniel Roberts, a PhD in soil science, studied at the University of New Hampshire before getting into the wine industry and becoming a prominent viticulture consultant in California. "There's nothing more destructive to terroir than winemaking,"[21] he says. The example all parties generally agree on is a wine that's been so heavily oaked as to obliterate any subtlety of fruit under a tide of wood flavor. Further examples of typicity's end might be a bag of industrial tannin, a de-alcoholizing machine or a dollop of the grape concentrate product Mega Purple.

Though it is difficult to find credible wine authorities who defend the coexistence of terroir with the evidence of highly impactful winemaking in the same glass, opinions begin to differ once winemaking practices are delimited by what has been practiced traditionally. A thought experiment may help elucidate the dividing line. In regions where the use of new oak has a long history and is argued to be helpful in managing the heavy tannins of the wine, can this ever be seen as part of terroir? Some might argue that oak aging is sacrosanct to the local culture and if all the local wines have this unique identifying typicity then it is part of terroir. Others who define terroir according to only environmental features would argue that oak aging might be part of tradition and typicity but that it is not part of terroir.

Another sub-debate within the winemaker's impact on terroir revolves around the use of yeast. Some winemakers claim that using native yeast – that is, the practice of relying on the ambient yeast population to start a fermentation – is more likely to create a wine of terroir because commercially purchased yeast imparts a distinct profile on the wine. One might argue that any profile that is not from the vineyard should be seen as an affront, thwarting Mother Nature and jumbling any sense of place.

After Louis Pasteur's 1857 discovery that the fungus, yeast, carried out alcoholic fermentation, vintners emerged from a world in which they had not understood the causal mechanism of the very product that sustained them and entered into a world in which previously unimaginable innovation was possible. Researchers went on to discover different strains of yeast, the conditions that these yeasts thrived or died in, and the unique aromas that they created. In the modern age, vintners have at their disposal an arsenal of yeast options, along with the understanding of how to create the conditions for certain native yeasts to thrive.

Critics contend that purchased yeast is an additive that removes the sense of place. Others push back on this claim, arguing that not intervening often creates a wine that is even less respectful of terroir. If a winemaker takes juice from the same vineyard and places it in different vessels it's possible for different yeasts to dominate the fermentation, changing the rich, chemical ecosystems to taste radically differently. One vessel might have been dominated by a yeast called *Kloeckera*, producing ethyl acetate, which smells like nail polish remover. Another vessel could be dominated by a yeast called *Brettanomyces*, which generally produces aromas that many describe as barnyard or sweaty socks. A third vessel might be taken over by *Acetobacter*, a bacteria that produces a vinegar aroma. This camp argues that all these wines would exhibit off-odors, making it difficult to determine any sense of place from any of them.

The vintners that push back against microbial anarchy are often still in favor of native yeast. They just favor using techniques that encourage desirable native yeast types, like *Saccharomyces cerevisiae*, because it allows for a pure taste. This would mean that controlling juice temperature and adding a nitrogen source and other proper nutrition to the juice would be fair interventions in the service of terroir. Others argue that there are plenty of neutral tasting commercial yeasts that cannot be told apart from the native *Saccharomyces cerevisiae*. Accepting any of these viewpoints would mean that winemaking is not solely destructive, and that winemakers can act as the shepherds of terroir, herding the chemical players into the right places at the right times. There are a huge number of winemaking interventions, some traditional, some new, and the position of the line where terroir ends and concoction begins continues to confound the wine trade and public alike.

The intervention question does not begin and end with winemaking though. There are choices within vineyards that intelligent minds have disagreed over. Daniel Roberts takes aim at terraforming, the practice of dramatically reshaping land or moving different soils to ready a site for a vineyard. "Whatever terroir had to do with topography, they annihilated it completely,"[22] he says of an ambitious terraforming project in Napa. This argument, typical of a widespread view, positions nature as an important element of terroir. A site may be planted, but the soil and topography must not be overly manipulated.

Europe has a long history of reshaping the land. In the 1600s, Dutch engineers added drainage channels to a marshland, allowing it to be planted. This region was the Médoc in Bordeaux. If the work was carried out today some might argue that this engineering feat negated terroir, but since the reshaping occurred so long ago many do not view this historical event as permanently canceling terroir. The Burgundy-based wine writer Jasper Morris brought up the example of a grower who carted soil from the highway up to his *premier cru* vineyard. Upon hearing of this, the authorities had the *premier cru* status removed from the site. Morris clarifies his views that for wine regions where hierarchy is built on the premise of terroir, "if you change that terroir you ought to be disqualified from your particular classification."[23] With that said he makes clear that in his mind, that fallen site nonetheless expresses its place. "It's still terroir, you've just changed the terroir."[24] For people who view terroir as an expression of nature through wine, these sorts of interventions might ring foul, but for those with less naturalistic inclinations, they might be just as fine with adjusted ground.

Indeed, all land is adjusted from nature for farming, so debaters must consider where their comfort levels lie and where the line should be drawn. Daniel Brunier of Domaine du Vieux Télégraphe in the Rhône is on the record as stating that "We cannot call [it] terroir if it's irrigated or drained."[25] This perspective likely arises from the naturalist principle whereby the way to honor a site is by letting it stand the way it would in nature without intervening. Greg Jones takes the other approach. "The idea that you can't have terroir if you irrigate is a little shallow."[26] Some who reject Brunier's argument might call it the naturalist fallacy. Others would point to the absurdity of stating that agriculture, a fundamentally unnatural imposition on an ecosystem, can ever be natural. If irrigation is not allowed, then why allow compost or fertilizer which similarly changes how the soil functions vis-à-vis the plant. Others could point to weed control, pruning, canopy management and a host of activities that make grapes from a vineyard distinctly different from wild grapevines.

Still, someone holding on to a particularly naturalistically inclined interpretation of terroir could respond with a *reductio ad absurdum* example showcasing where a perspective of terroir that accepts any farming changes might go – a vine growing in a pot within the controlled environment of a greenhouse stretches most people's conceptions of what a place of terroir can and should be. This serves to prove that the line between natural and unnatural terroir needs to be drawn somewhere and if irrigation is a significant enough impact to alter the flavor profile of the fruit[27] then it might as well be drawn there.

The skeptics can clap back however, volleying the straw man fallacy; of course, it is possible to overwater and negatively impact a wine, but not all waterers commit this sin. That the argument hints at exclusivity also makes the critic question to what extent terroir is being circumscribed to cut out certain wineries and regions from using the term to increase the profit and social hierarchy of the haves over the have-nots.

Another farming input topic is that of the rootstock, the underground, root part of the vine, which is then usually grafted to *Vitis vinifera*. A question sometimes asked is to what degree rootstock choice is an intervention that alters terroir and changes a wine's profile. The discipline of matching plant material to soil type is not something that can be done by gut intuition, with years of knowledge to view how vineyards fared being the only way to understand how to find success. Daniel Roberts has dealt with many rootstocks in his career and can deftly describe their best uses, as well as their quirks. "GRN-1 [a rootstock] has the worst magnesium deficiency on the planet, but I just use Epsom salts – so what? People say, well, that's not terroir. I say, really? You can't farm without fertilizing anything, regardless of what it is."[28] Roberts hints at the core tenet of the debate, which much like the irrigation debate comes back to the amorphous idea of how close to nature it is possible or desirable to get.

The list of other possible terroir-impacting farming and winemaking decisions goes on and on. What about selecting the clone for the grape? Some clones have higher or lower acid than others, even in the same soil. Does this pervert a natural sense of place? How about fining (the addition of egg whites to red wines to clarify the wine and soften the tannins)? Many winemakers have done this for centuries. Does this softening of mouthfeel betray the idea of place? Or should it be accepted if it's been common practice for a long time, as in Bordeaux?

Perhaps the easiest jumping off point is to define a terroir wine by what it's not. If a wine of terroir is one you can guess the location by tasting blind, a wine without terroir is one you drink and have no idea where it's from at all. In some cases – oak use – it can be quite easy to taste the intervention in question, but in others it can be impossible. And if one can taste the fruit and get a sense of place but there is one flavor running through the middle of the wine screaming intervention, does that disqualify the wine from the sacred designation of place?

The last and most amorphous question about what to include in terroir is the cultural practices. The historian Philip Whalen has documented the attempt to link French cultural value to the concept of terroir: "In interwar Burgundy, Gabriel Jeanton and Gaston Roupnel stand out in the development of modern conceptions of terroir and in efforts to '(re)cover' and anchor (both geographically and culturally) an essentialized, rustic, and traditional cultural identity that could provide an alternative to generic models of 'modern,' anonymous, urban, and bureaucratic national French identity."[29]

Whalen goes on to catalogue the use of Burgundian cultural events and practices as integral to terroir. In this sense, by drinking a wine of terroir the consumer was not merely partaking of the purity of nature, but imbibing the cultural history of France. Marion Demossier, the French anthropologist, has noted that terroir is valued not just because of any discernible taste differences but because the act of production is "fabrication in a time-honored fashion."[30] Some might argue this notion is appropriate for the word, while others could reject it as not being narrowly tailored to the original naturalistic idea.

If this cultural dimension is accepted, it becomes easier to exclude places, suggesting that terroir wines only come from places with that cultural history. If terroir is just the collective natural elements that constitute a place and nurture the grape into what it is on a physicochemical level, then it's simple to argue that everyone has it. But with the cultural trappings included, it's easier to state that not everyone can make a terroir wine. Benjamin Bois, a researcher at the University of Dijon, adjusts the definition of terroir in this way: "So, it becomes terroir when you decide to build an identity so the consumers can say, okay, this is the taste of the place."[31] This organizing theory would allow for, and even encourage, state intervention in farming and winemaking rules, and justify jettisoning rule-breaking wines that have microbially-derived funky aromas, like volatile acidity. How recognizable an identity must be for it to become terroir according to this reading is up for further discussion, if this standard is one everyone would be willing to accept at all.

* * *

As the concept of terroir turns from purely scientific to sociological, it leads to the next big question: to what extent is terroir a meaningful and legitimate concept and to what extent is it more of a marketing tool? Put another way, if someone tells you a wine expresses terroir, should you care?

Terroir certainly has its educated critics. Dr. Mark Matthews, a plant physiologist in the department of viticulture at UC Davis, who wrote the book *Terroir and Other Myths of Winegrowing*, hardly conceals his skepticism for the idea. Business scholars have noted that claiming to make a product that cannot be copied using other soils acts as a barrier to entry to anyone trying to make the same product.[32]

The food historian Rachel Laudan has written dismissively of terroir, suggesting that the shifting term was used by marketers to prop up French wine against competition. Phylloxera is a sap-sucking insect that wiped out huge swaths of European vineyards in the second half of the 1800s. As a solution to the scourge, most European grapevines were grafted onto American rootstocks, which were immune. Because of this, Laudan reports, there was a fear that the vines would not be seen as special, so another justification was needed to boost sales: "With this market-threatening possibility in mind, the growers argued that it was not the vines themselves that made French wine so good. It was the terroir. Terroir, first defined as the soil, quickly came to mean the local environment in which wine was produced."[33]

Marion Demossier expands on this idea; noting that the cultural circumstances often overshadow any objective superiority of viticulture, she prefers to think of terroir as mistaken "geological determinism,"[34] whereas "elites and wealthy landowners sought to empower themselves at different historical periods by taking into their hands the ideology of terroir and moving it forward in relation to their changing economic situation."[35] It would be distasteful to many that elites may be baking into the idea of terroir the imagery of the historic working peasantry in order to valorize and then profit from the land. It is because of this that she calls terroir a "strategically deployed myth," and notes "at the end of the day the terroir is delineated by the piece of land you've inherited or you own and it's an artificial construction – it's an historical construction – and nothing to do with taste or better quality."[36] In this way terroir can operate to determine societal and economic power, entrenching and exacerbating the differences between the people who have and don't have the most respected plots of land.

Olivier Jacquet, a historian of wine and the UNESCO Chair in Wine Culture and Traditions at the Université Bourgogne Europe, has researched the history of French terroir and the laws surrounding it extensively. He is sanguine about the use of terroir as a marketing tool:

There was a striking moment, the moment of the Judgment of Paris in 1976, where this time the French wines were beaten by the Californian wines and we effectively begin to see foreign competition ... Starting at this moment, especially in the 1980s, there was another discourse on terroir which appeared less and less rational – more and more ideological. And in particular, one saw appearing the idea that the monks tasted the earth, that we were bringing back the terroir of the Middle Ages. Effectively all of this had the objective of saying, "Voila, we have a place that is inimitable, that is untransportable in the world, and is a way to compete with the new competition."[37]

Given this case against terroir, not only are wineries wrong about its effects, they are culpable in misrepresenting the truth about what makes good wine.

What's a defender of terroir to say? Even those who acknowledge that the term can be used as an economic weapon to ward off competition can admit that there is still truth in the core idea. The way to prove this is to show that terroir is sensorially real – that it is not just a fiction made up by elites to make money. Blind tasting, the most obvious method of telling the difference between two terroirs, suffers from human fallibility, but the ability of certain tasters to blind guess wine correctly at levels above random chance would in theory prove that these differences are real.

The next attempted proof of terroir comes from the research community. Recent scientific work has tried to shine light on the concept by measuring trace elements in wines to see if certain regions leave a chemical signature. One of the most compelling studies was undertaken by researchers from UC Davis and Pennsylvania State University. They hypothesized that it would be possible to tell the differences not just between wines from different countries or regions, but from different climates within one region: the Russian River Valley in Sonoma County, California.

Over two harvests, 2015 and 2017, the researchers measured a minimum of 60 elements, using wine collected from wineries at an early stage (before much winemaking could change the results). The researchers noted, "Taken together, the elemental differences in the wines originating from the different neighborhoods are generally stable across vintages, indicating consistent overall elemental fingerprints."[38] In addition to scientific studies, there is a litany of anecdotal examples of vintners growing the same clone of the grape across neighboring plots and it's possible to taste a difference. In cases where the soil is different, this would help to show that the concept did not come from nowhere. It's possible to acknowledge that some throughout history have used the concept in nakedly profit-driven ways, but there is a strong case, it's argued, that the concept is not magic but a real phenomenon.

There is some pushback from the anti-terroir faction. Blind tasters may base their answers on winemaking styles, which might be distinct from terroir. Trace elements that can be measured with advanced laboratory equipment might not be able to be detected by humans. And to this proponents argue back that people can and do detect these elements as demonstrated by the robust blind tasting around the world.

* * *

Given what we know about the differences between wines grown in different places, the question to terroirists remains: Why is it valued? Why should the average consumer care? Amy Trubek, an anthropologist focusing on food studies at the University of Vermont and the author of a book on terroir, *Taste the Place*, has an answer. "There is no way that we can understand what terroir means without understanding the fact that it's a call to a concept of nature and locale in a time where people do not live locally based lives."[39] In a globalizing world, people are looking for connection, tradition, and uniqueness within corporate homogeneity, and if terroir can give it to them, that is a good thing. In this sense, terroir offers to the consumer a sense of authenticity in liquid form – individuality and character in a sea of sameness.

The wine trade places a heavy focus on terroir as a unifying theory to understand wine, with books, certificates, and courses based on the premise. Many people marvel at the differences between vineyards under the belief that place is the transcendent explanation. Perhaps part of the reason that the idea holds power is because people are creating and consuming a product that celebrates place. They form communities around these ideals which then become part of their identities as human beings.

Still, as the ethnologist and cultural anthropologist Rajko Muršič has observed, "Any experience of authenticity is at the same time a building block of a social exclusion."[40] When practitioners glorify some land at the expense of another, skeptical consumers might wonder if the slight is really due to a difference in merit or is just mirroring commercial hierarchy. For some, this sort of behavior is akin to a culture war that isn't that meaningful to begin with. Plants behave differently in different places and it's possible to notice those differences through taste – for some this just isn't that big of a deal.

But for the advocates, the terroirists, the pursuit of the idea of naturalness and purity is something they can't let go of. As Amy Trubek observes, "In the end, it remains compelling because we're still meditating on the very fundamental concept of humanity versus nature."[41] To the extent that it's possible to attain a sense of nature in a product, this inspires devotion in those who follow it. Skeptics are within their rights to question any exercise of purity as puritanical performance and such movements frequently have downsides. As long as the terroir question opens a conversation about how to define what is natural, how to define what is pure and the possibility of sensing or determining timeless culture, it will continue to fascinate the wine world.

2
Rules of wine regions – the liquid codification of geography

"What region of the earth is not full of our calamities?"

Virgil

Along the old pilgrimage road to the Spanish holy city of Santiago de Compostela lies the ancient French town of Saint-Émilion. The town's beautiful stone churches remain as testament to its monastic significance, helping to justify its UNESCO status. Today, those who make a pilgrimage to the town are more likely to come for its wine, praying at the altars of Merlot and Cabernet Franc, the two grapes that constitute the backbone of the regional blend.

However, behind the curtains of this miracle of stone, earth and vines, there is trouble in paradise. The system of ranking its wines, begun in 1955, has held firm since its inception, despite the fact that the system allows for a re-ranking of estates every decade or so. The re-evaluations of the estates have been raucously controversial since the turn of the century, with pressure building until the 2022 reclassification, when three of the top ranked estates voluntarily stepped down from the system in protest.

One of these highest ranked denizens of Bordeaux's right bank is a winery called Château Cheval Blanc. Closed to the public, its long, tree-lined entrance leads to a lake, a nineteenth-century greenhouse, and an ornate winery, all surrounded by a sea of vines. Arnaud de Laforcade, the commercial director of Cheval Blanc, reflects on the last 70 years of rules surrounding the wine classification system that placed Cheval Blanc, along with nearby Château Ausone, at the top for most of the system's history. On the one hand he notes that there is no dream classification. On the other hand he believes it's not possible to re-evaluate terroir.[1]

Laforcade is alluding to the question at the heart of the debate. If wine should be judged by its terroir, and terroir is permanent and unchanging, then re-evaluating that terroir should have no place in the system, or so the advocates would argue. Yet, if no system of ranking and ordering can be perfect, at what point should wine regions stop trying? Laforcade suggests that the reason the system worked for so long was because since its inception the rankings didn't change, affirming a unified idea of terroir.

Those cynical of changes note that allowing regions to change their status in re-evaluations invites the possibility for big marketing budgets to hold more sway, the same logic that many in the political arena use to justify strong, hard-to-change constitutions.

In 2022 the classification changed its standards for what accounted for a Premier Grand Cru Classé wine, with "reputation" accounting for 35 percent of the score, a category that includes "advertising, distribution and value."[2] "We would have had to get an Instagram account,"[3] complains Laforcade about one of the myriad sub-rules. Anyone with a robust marketing budget could eventually get full points in this category, implying that money, not land, is the coin of the realm in Saint-Émilion. Both Cheval Blanc and Château Ausone dropped out of the Saint-Émilion classification, a clear act of protest.

Though some were critical of the changes that the regional body made, others could see logic to the rules. In order to be a member in good standing, wineries need to do their part to represent the region well. Not only that, but many would suggest that a permanent hierarchy of ranked wineries was not compatible with a reality where the quality and reputation of domaines can change with time.

Regardless of the issue at hand, the story of Saint-Émilion is a microcosm of the question faced by others in the wine world. When a winery or grower disagrees with the local rules, how is this conflict resolved? How are the rules decided on to begin with? And should the state even play a strong role in the world of wine?

* * *

Rules controlling winemaking date back at least to ancient Rome,[4] but the eighteenth century saw a new push for more specific rules. The Tuscan regions of Chianti and Carmignano were demarcated in 1716 by Medici Grand Duke Cosimo II of Florence, and in the mid-1700s the Douro region of Portugal was born when the Marquis de Pombal created boundaries as well as production rules for wines made there to ensure quality was maintained.[5] As the twentieth century dawned, the trajectory that wine rules were heading along would be irrevocably altered. Olivier Jacquet, a historian at the University of Burgundy, suggests that the Italians and Spanish worked on wine rules but because of fascism, progress stalled and, as he concludes, "it was France that took the leadership on this."[6]

In 1905, in response to the practice of passing off general wines as wines from a specific place, France passed a law intended to stop the fraudulent labeling of wines. This was only the first step, since the changes were not seen as enough. In 1907, over half a million southern French citizens protested, some of them dying in the rioting, to demand change for how wine was regulated. A new law soon followed in 1908 that officially codified wine regions.

These various protections culminated in the Statut Viticole of 1935, which established the appellation of origin (AOC) system for the entire country. In addition to the clarification of labeling issues, one of the other motivations behind these regulatory changes included a desire to limit competition coming from Algeria, which the French government was attempting to assimilate.[7] The majority of French vignerons, however, made clear that competition was not appreciated, and programs were developed to avoid overproduction of grapes to control prices. One of the most lasting policy implications was restricting which grape varieties were permitted.[8]

This was not the first attempt at international intellectual property writ large – language about appellation of origin made it into the Paris Convention of 1883, which covered much broader issues of international trade.[9] In 1891, the Madrid Agreement pushed further, permitting seizure for products that included deceptive language about their origin.[10] These original flutterings of protection were lax enough that ideas of place in wine were far from set in stone, in part because they didn't need to be; without mass transit, local wines didn't need to be protected because most wine was local.

Apart from deciding where to draw boundaries and which grapes went in which regions, adultery and dilution became questions that wine region policymakers had to address. Any region that grew in reputation faced the temptation of increasing volume by adding in grapes from nearby regions or adjusting with non-vinous ingredients. Similarly, a region that attained reputational renown could be undone by some producers free-riding on the success of their neighbors, charging a premium for the regional name but placing cheap plonk in the bottles. This collective action problem promised to undermine any region that attained success, and authorities decided the state could get involved to solve the problem.

* * *

The history of wine production in the United States brought about a different approach to defining and refining regional rules. No legal place boundaries existed, so every grower could make his own interpretation of what to include and what not to include.[11] The permissiveness in regions extended to labeling in general, with the European settlers often naming their wines after the places where they were from.

While 1920s France was a hotbed of thought on how to better regulate wine, in America, teetotalers were raising the flag of victory. Grape bricks, the Prohibition-era product made from concentrated grapes shaped into a bar – which consumers could add water to and ferment into wine as a loophole around Prohibition rules – likely did not spur drinkers to opine deeply about the importance of the terroir from which it came.

Emerging from Prohibition with the Twenty-first Amendment in 1933, the United States maintained the less restrictive land-based regulations, until rumblings came from across the pond. In short, Europeans wanted ex-Europeans to stop using European place names, and the best way to achieve this was to convince countries around the world to adopt their own place-based restrictions so that local names could be used instead. While Europeans thought this was a natural and obvious solution, to many European immigrants who had left and settled in other winegrowing regions, this didn't seem right.

Nevertheless, Americans set out to create their own wine region rules, the American Viticultural Area (AVA) system, and Americans discovered the painful process the French had already gone through: drawing boundaries. In the region north of the San Francisco and San Pablo Bays, Napa County contained several valleys, including Wooden Valley, Gordon Valley, Napa Valley, Pope Valley, and Chiles Valley. Historically, grapes from all of these regions had gone into Napa Valley wines. Indeed, there was a history in the north bay of combining grapes from Sonoma, Mendocino, Napa, and Lake Counties into the same wines. So, with a blank slate, the borders of AVAs could have been drawn anywhere.

Different factions gathered to argue about where the lines should be drawn for an emerging Napa AVA, some wanting all of Napa County's valleys under one AVA, with others wanting the site to be only Napa Valley, excluding the other valleys. There was a proposal to create two AVAs, Napa Valley and Napa Mountain, for the reason that mountain fruit going into a wine with "Valley" in the name would confuse consumers. Much was made of the Pacific Telephone Company's decision to change how Napa was referred to in the phone book from Napa County to Napa Valley – this was taken as proof that the wider region was known to the general public as a valley and therefore this common usage should be used on the basis of public understanding.[12] Ultimately the place known as Napa Valley came to be several valleys as well as mountains, an example of the compromise that would be typical of other regions.

Glenn McGourty, based in northern California's Mendocino County, comments on how it feels to work in an underdog wine region: "We've always been in this funny position where people know the fruit's good, and they like blending [with it] because the costs are good too, but I always described it as being like a hot date you want to go out with, but you don't want your parents to know about."[13] This dynamic is at the heart of the exclusionist question – if the state excludes an underdog that has good quality fruit, is it complicit in unfair treatment?

This touchy question of who to include and who to exclude begs the question of whether any government should intervene in niche wine policy at all. Particularly in places with strong brand names, like Sonoma or Napa, government intervention regarding where to draw a line is necessarily an act of picking winners and losers. Draw the line too loosely and the consumer is at a loss because the region is too large to have an identity and there's no marketability. Draw the line too tightly and two neighbors that make stylistically similar wines might face very different realities, and the policy goal of helping farmers make a living is for nought. Landowners know the power of more closely limiting a famous name to a small number of elite other names and can lobby for this to occur, with other monied interests lobbying to widen borders to include certain plots. The act of drawing these difficult wine region barriers is what the historical geographer Tim Unwin has called the "delimitation of privilege."[14] In wine, drawing borders is deciding power.

In addition to where to draw boundaries, a second question emerges as to whether a government should ever help adjudicate a tiered system of vineyard quality. Much like a food pyramid organizes food, the hierarchy of regional place has created an unofficial wine pyramid – country or regional blends make up the everyday wine base of the pyramid, more specific sub-regions rest on top of that, and at the top of the pyramid lie the site-specific wines. The classic example is Burgundy, where there are four tiers: Bourgogne, village wines, *premier cru* and *grand cru*. Around the world vintners and writers have attempted to find better sites, equivalent or similar to *grands crus*, but should the market or the government choose which vineyards are the best? And if the government chooses, how much can we trust it to make objective decisions?

The anthropologist Marion Demossier has written that at the inception of the Burgundian wine hierarchy by the state, "The AOC and terroir ideology constructed by the wine elites reflected the existing social hierarchy but it worked to the advantage of many ordinary peasants, although their exclusion from the AOC negotiations meant that those with plots in the wrong places risked marginalization."[15] One of the critiques of the system of hierarchical rules is that the hierarchy of taste is not self-evident from nature, and it's not even the state's honest attempt to differentiate quality, it is a way in which producers are able to use the state to justify their superiority, and thus their ability to charge a premium for their wines.[16]

The question many regions will face is whether they will ever reach a point in history where it is possible to correctly categorize more worthwhile and less worthwhile sites. One of the theories explaining how France was able to pass a system of laws codifying a hierarchy of quality in regions like Burgundy was because of the aristocratic and royal history that allowed for taste to be defined by the state.[17] This contrasts sharply with other governing traditions where this might not have been possible. So this question is more theoretical than practical at this point. Nonetheless, the allure of determining which sites are better and whether the government should be tasked with enforcing that hierarchy is another implicit disagreement baked into the differing rules of wine regions that occasionally gives us cause to think.

* * *

While both the French and the Americans had to wrestle with the difficulty of how to draw borders, the American system of AVAs developed to be particularly lax, not requiring certain grape varieties, yields, irrigation practices, hierarchies, or cultural protections. Many around the world developed similar, more laissez-faire models arguing that greater freedom was best for growers.

Back in Europe, the system developed in much more rigorous ways in part to account for and protect cultural as well as economic interests. Andrea Zappalaglio, an Italian legal scholar based at the University of Leeds in the United Kingdom, who specializes in intellectual property and geographical indication law, explains the developing tension: "When it comes to Europe, the idea is that the GI [geographic indicator] is the intellectual property right meant to protect heritage, meant to support rural development, meant to protect rural communities – local communities. On the other side of the Atlantic, it has become this kind of intellectual property right invented by the Europeans to screw the Americans."[18]

In defense of the diaspora, in America as well as other non-European places, geographic names were often seen more as a style of wine, not as a place on a map, and using these names was the clearest means of communicating wine style to a consumer. This practice made all the more sense because in the 1800s in Europe, place names were not yet firmly regulated either, so the immigrants making wines in new lands were functionally using the names with the same permissiveness that they were used to before. And given that the styles of wines often varied in Europe within one region, the fact that the new wine also varied felt less like a stylistic betrayal and more like a natural evolution of these old terms. Lastly, the bigger difference between the regions was not the place, but the blending choices.

Europeans, in the name of terroir, cried foul upon learning of these wines, their grievances sharpened by the fact that some New World wines barely shared any commonalities with their original namesakes. There needed to be protection against lax New World producers using a place name with no intention of honoring the tradition or style of the wine. To them, calling a Zinfandel blend Tuscan was theft, pure and simple, and if that could happen, the Europeans had a strong argument that stringent legal protections were required to defend the cultural history that is wine.

The implicit question is to what degree geography should supersede cultural lineage as the sole guarantor of place and how closely to guard that name. The first response from the Europeans is to point to terroir – making wine from the same grapes in the same way in a different place does not create the same product because of soil, climate, and other difficult to define geographic variables. In this sense, it doesn't matter if an Australian or Argentinian family has centuries of Tuscan lineage and all the winemaking know-how. In wine law, soil is thicker than blood.

How closely to protect those names was another question regulators had to contend with. As time passed and after international treaties were signed largely limiting the right to use place names to those places, there were some who suggested that the rules were drawn particularly tight, going beyond protecting identities and into protectionism. In reviewing both sides of the case, Zappalaglio summarizes a critique of the laws as they were written, "Geographical indications in Europe are protected against pretty much anything, even if there is no confusion, even if there is no deception, even if no one mentally sane would ever say that there is an infringement."[19]

For example, a wine that in small print on the back label describes itself as "Alsatian-style" or "inspired by the blends of Bordeaux" would be against the rules even if the bottle stated in large, all-capital letters "produced and bottled in South Africa." Zappalaglio notes that a Chicago restaurant can advertise and sell Neapolitan-style pizzas, but if they were using the standards of wine, this would not be allowed. A critic of GI law as it's written can argue that they were taken too far, that they do not create more transparent information for consumers, and that the rules are mostly about protecting the profits of European wineries.

Other critics argue that the European Union (EU) has sometimes overstepped, pushing protectionism too far. The case study of Prosecco is a key example of disagreement. Italians wished to get protected status for the sparkling wine they produced from the Prosecco grape. They renamed the variety Glera, allowing them to use the village of Prosecco as the basis for gaining protected regional status for the wine. But Prosecco was already grown and produced in other parts of the world, particularly in Australia. Kym Anderson, an Australian professor emeritus of economics who, amongst other things, has written the history of the globalization of wine, argues that this was unfair:

> It's got no legal legitimacy at all, other than it's being accepted in the EU, but in terms of WTO [World Trade Organization] type practice of law at least, it would be seen as an illegal move to suddenly turn a variety into a region name and then protect that region name and say, "you therefore can't use it as a variety." I mean, it's never happened before. This is a new example of exploiting a legal potential loophole in the EU.[20]

Andrea Zappalaglio defends the Italian position, noting that according to the TRIPS agreement (the Agreement on Trade-Related Aspects of Intellectual Property Rights of 1995) it is not possible to name a grape the same as a region, so the Italians, stuck with Prosecco from Prosecco, were forced to change the name, and they chose to rename the grape. He points out that if the region of Champagne were making wine from a Champagne grape they would have been forced into the same choice. But making a more cultural point beyond the law, he argues the following:

> *So in Europe, there is no doubt that Prosecco wine belongs to a specific area in northeast Italy ... From a U.S. perspective, this is protectionism. From a European perspective, this is just what it is. No one in Europe would ever buy the argument you can make Prosecco in Australia. You can make sparkling wine, which is similar to Prosecco, and call it something else.*[21]

Felix Addor, the Deputy Director General and General Counsel at the Swiss Federal Institute of Intellectual Property, also defends European GI law, suggesting that without it real harms could be caused to European wine regions and vintners:

> *In particular, I would like to point out that the risk of genericization is very high for GIs, as demonstrated by geographical names that have become generic, such as Cheddar, Gouda or Frankfurt (sausages). This is why the only way to effectively protect GIs, and to ensure that consumers are not misled about quality and origin, is to forbid any mention of a GI on products that do not meet the required conditions to benefit from that GI, even accompanied by a disclaimer.*[22]

From this perspective, for GI apologists, no matter how small the writing or how clear the verbiage, the risk of commodification and cheapening is too great. The rules are justified.

Those who are fine with the fact that the cheddar cheese is not limited to the English west-country village of Cheddar might be more open to looser rules for wine, though the distinction with wine is whether terroir changes the dynamic. The specific process for how to make the cheese, known as cheddaring, was deemed of key importance, and that method spread around the world before protections were put in place.[23] Though some west-country cheesemakers contend the conditions of certain regional caves justify protections, the counterargument that has won out in some cases is that temperature and humidity levels in storage can be recreated, which means there isn't enough of a link to place.

With wine, with its strong assertion that place determines product, the argument for protecting place has been more strongly favored than for most other artisanal food products. If pizza was not a perishable good and could be bottled and sent around the world, would the Neapolitans have argued that the tomatoes, cheese and flour were unique to Naples and that pizzas made with other agricultural products were not close enough and were harmful to its people and reputation? It is the fact that wine can be bottled and sent around the world that has permitted the geographic indicator debate to occur.

The gustatory manifestation of terroir, regionally distinctive taste, is therefore the acid test to determine which theory should govern the geography versus cultural know-how debate – if regional wines can be consistently differentiated from their stylistic brethren, then geography is king, but if regional wines cannot be consistently identified, then the system is vulnerable to its critics.

One such critic was Timothy Josling, a Stanford agricultural economist who argued that the link to place needs to be not only plausible, but rock solid. He wrote, "… if the link between quality and location is not so reliable then the information may deflect choice and instead provide marketing advantage to one group of producers by restricting competition."[24] Following this argument, consumers are let down by overly high prices for unjustifiably protected place-name products. So, a critic might ask, What if the product, like cheddar, happens to be named after the region? If it is the production method, or in the case of wine, the blend that is of key importance for its distinction, some would argue that it doesn't deserve government protection from competition. The answer to this question depends on the power of terroir.

A related question is that if the climate changes dramatically over time due to global warming and as a result regions develop a new stylistic profile because of warmer weather, does that undermine the terroir tie? For example, if the historic mean average temperature of Champagne from over 50 years ago changes, and now a cooler region, such as Sussex in the UK, has a mean temperature the same as Champagne's former mean average temperature, even if the wines coming from Sussex aren't the same as old Champagne, does this shift undermine the argument that one geographically defined place will be the only place that can make a product in a particular way? Zappalaglio, reflecting on this question, opines on the underlying assumptions of what a geographic indicator is:

> *Unfortunately – being a European creation – they were designed to join places and culture, taking as understood – taking for granted – that the two things are the same, or anyway they physically overlap. It's really hard to say what will happen. Of course, I am in favor, and probably someday I will write a paper on the fact that we need cultural indications. The problem is always then how you identify the rights.*[25]

If climate change continues and Sussex wine is more like old Champagne than Champagne will be in the future, what should be the policy goal of wine region rules? One option, discussed by Zappalaglio in the context of Parma ham, is that the region just goes away – terms of trade could dictate that the product 'Champagne' ceases to exist because it no longer tastes like itself. Another option would be to change the idea of what Champagne is, expanding the term to include cooler climate regions like England, Tasmania, Patagonia, or others because Champagne is no longer defensibly unique.

Others argue that even if climate change affects some aspects of the product, its identity is tied more to cultural history, people and site, and so Champagne should continue to be the only legal Champagne. In this reading, Champagne's Champagneness resides in its traditions and cultural know-how, even if it is different than it was in the past. These are the legal ramifications of climate change – for a deeper discussion of the possible effects of climate change see Chapter 5.

* * *

Part of what separates wine from widgets in international trade is that as a cultural good, the relative successes or failures in the market can be seen as a culture war. In 2001, the French Minister of Agriculture stated, "Until recent years, wine was with us, we were the center, the unavoidable reference point. Today, the barbarians are at our gates: Australia, New Zealand, the United States, Chile, Argentina, South Africa."[26] A French vigneron commented, "Each bottle of American and Australian wine that lands in Europe is a bomb targeted at the heart of our rich European culture."[27] Though these statements cannot be misconstrued to represent the feelings of all Europeans, they indicate the underlying passion that fuels rulemaking around regional wine protection.

Preserving traditional ways of making wine is part of what justifies protecting wine regions through law. Whether it be UNESCO status or appellation designations, the idea is that sanctifying a region's methods of production in law encourages producers to continue the traditional way of making wine, which is a benefit to the region and the world as a whole. Richard Mendelson, Director of the Wine Law and Policy Program and a senior research fellow at UC Berkeley, who has argued wine law in front of the California Supreme Court, suggests that with geographic indicators "you are protecting culture and you're protecting terroir as part of cultural practices and standards, not just the natural environment."[28]

Tomer Broude, a legal scholar of Public and International Law at the Hebrew University of Jerusalem Faculty of Law, argues that despite a belief that geographic indicators protect tradition, "their effect on cultural preservation and diversity is indeterminate at best. This is because GI protected traditions might nevertheless in the future succumb to economic pressures and international consumer preferences."[29] He cites the movement in Tuscany away from Italianate grapes and towards Bordelais grapes as an example. What protects regional history is not their laws, but their ability to capitalize on their traditional products. Regulatory artifice follows market reality. The moment a region can make more money by discontinuing a tradition, people will abandon tradition in favor of the more lucrative route.

A host of vignerons would rise up in opposition to the view expressed by Broude. Acts of rebellion by the few do not indicate a loss of culture by the many. Additionally, by clarifying production methods and standard tastes, consumers better know what to expect and are more likely to buy the wines. Producers can use this money to invest in making even better wine, creating a harmonious upward cycle. It's been argued that in Piedmont, by choosing the more restrictive Protected Designation of Origin (PDO) instead of the looser Indicazione Geografica Tipica (IGT) standard, the region better grew the quality of its wines.[30]

Part of what allows protected regions to maintain a cultural practice, is not that it is merely enshrined in law, but that the traditional practice meant something to begin with. This begs the question how the rules in practice have operated and if all applications for PDOs have equal cultural merit. Bernard O'Connor, a European lawyer and author who specializes in geographic indicator law, notes, "I think some of these new applications ... probably should have been subject to a greater scrutiny."[31]

Zappalaglio warns of ghost GIs, noting that "You can have, for instance, the mayor of a small city, a little town somewhere, who in 1995 thought it was a good idea, and registered a GI essentially without telling anyone. This is the best way to fail because the successful GIs usually are the result of a bottom to top approach, not vice versa."[32] If true, it begs the question of whether PDO law as it is written is enshrining cultural heritage or allowing regions to piggyback on the successful idea of PDOs to prop up a less than significant cultural practice.

Defenders of the system can argue that poorly made PDOs are nonexistent, or at least very rare, and that even if there were small cracks in the system, that would not invalidate the foundation of a very good idea. The premise of protecting a region to preserve its culture still stands. The next question becomes to what degree culture is a static idea and to what extent it can change. Broude goes on with his argument: "As pressure mounts to establish international legal mechanisms of cultural protection that entail restrictions to trade, we must ask ourselves whether by curtailing economic human exchanges such mechanisms do not at the same time prevent human cultural exchanges in whose vibrancy lies the future of human cultural development and its diversity."[33]

In winegrowing regions without many rules, growers are free to experiment: in doing that work they have created products with their own sense of style unique from their European counterparts. Think of Hunter Valley Semillon, New Zealand Sauvignon Blanc, South African Chenin Blanc or Russian River Valley Pinot Noir. At what point do these wines cease to be innovations of grape and place and become local traditions and cultures? When should they be enshrined in law, if ever? And ought we not view these places as having living cultures that should be appreciated highly as well? Maybe culture can involve changing grape varieties more often rather than sticking with the current set for eternity?

* * *

One of the core questions at the heart of the wine region debate is how narrowly to restrict the grape varieties that can be planted and other farming decisions like crop yield and irrigation. In general, more restrictive regional rules come from Europe, with fewer restrictions elsewhere. Some countries, such as the United States or Australia, represent a laissez-faire approach to regional regulation. Other countries, like South Africa, have more exacting rules.[34]

Kevin Fandl, an American legal scholar, argues that the very rules intended to help the wine industry in Europe are in fact hurting it.

> *The heart of my thesis is that government regulations meant to protect wine quality may limit opportunities to adapt to changing consumer preferences in the wine export market.*

> *More precisely, the stricter the regulation, the less opportunity firms have to respond to changes in consumer demand through innovative techniques in the production and marketing of their products."*[35]

In this analysis, if global demand changed to appreciate one grape more than another – as was the case after the movie *Sideways* popularized Pinot Noir – a region whose name was tied to the use of a particular grape might not be able to adapt as quickly if at all. Regions unable to shift their grapes to what is in demand might suffer economically.

There have been several ripostes to this critique. Elizabeth Carter, an American professor who teaches, amongst other topics, food politics at the University of New Hampshire, professed to having this perspective, which she brought to her research interviews in France. "I had my first meeting with the Ministry of Agriculture. And I said, 'So, you know, your wine really hinders you. *Big* government. What are you going to do? You can't respond to demand.' And the guy looked at me and said, 'Our wines sell for the highest prices in the world *because* of our regulation, not in spite of it.'"[36]

This powerful response to Fandl's argument is in part the justification for a more strict regulatory regime. His school of economics is thinking too literally about what value to a consumer is, or so critics would argue. New yeasts, new grapes, new flavors and other economic innovations are not what wine consumers want – what matters when seeking great wine is to appreciate and enjoy places with authenticity, tradition, and identity. Rather than entering a wild west region full of all sorts of grapes, styles, and experiments, consumers want to know what they are buying. In the same way that the United States protects its National Parks, Europeans protect their cultural heritage through wine.

What's more, the defenders of these rules can argue that change is possible, it just happens at a slower pace and only once there is consensus in the region that the change will benefit everyone.

This isn't a set of handcuffs, it is an opportunity for reflection that allows for a vision of change that maintains the unity of a region's identity. This is important both for the wineries and for giving consumers what they actually want. Elizabeth Carter admitted to appreciating the European way of doing things much more after her visit.[37]

Still, some critics argue that a system slow to change is not able to respond quickly enough to allow for progressive environmental change. Modern grapes hybridized to have particular traits such as mildew resistance, which could mean a massive reduction in chemical vineyard spray application, were only allowed by the registered wine regions within the European Union in 2021.

Another example of adaptation to change potentially shackling European wine regions is water use. With climate change, there has arguably been an increase in the need to water vines to withstand heat, but some regions have been slow to allow watering. In some cases this reticence of rulemakers to change in the face of a shifting climate has arguably harmed vine health. In 2025 Château Lafleur announced it would be dropping out of the Pomerol appellation, citing concerns that the regional rulemaking was too slow to account for the droughts and heatwaves brought about by the changing climate. The defenders of a rules-based order for wine regions celebrate the wisdom of slow and deliberate change. Its critics suggest that slowness has become a straitjacket that permits the micromanagement of farming practices, limiting the freedom of the vintners within the system who know their land the best.

Lastly, there is a response at the heart of what the Minister of Agriculture said to Elizabeth Carter, that the ability to attain high prices is the defense and justification for a well-regulated system. Kym Anderson calls price a "crude indicator" of quality. "In Australia, the average retail price of wine has hardly changed in nominal dollar terms for 30 years yet the quality of that wine has gone up enormously ... So how you measure quality improvement, I don't know – given that it's certainly not reflected in price."[38] Rules might help some wineries get higher prices, but economists might suggest that good wine at a lower price is a better goal.

On that front, Europeans can defend themselves, pointing to a wide array of affordable, good quality entry level wines. Some economists might respond, suggesting that the massive government stimulus for agriculture helps this, but that is another debate for another book. On the larger point of wine region rules, the question is whether the rules as they are written balance innovation with a desirable sense of typicity.

* * *

In order to confirm that place confers a distinct taste, some wine regions have decided to ask that each wine bottle set to be sold under the regional name goes in front of a tasting committee to ensure that it is typical of the region. Italy created a tiered system of place with Denominazione di Origine Controllata e Garantita (DOCG) wines recognized as the most tied to regional place identity. DOCG wines in Italy must be tasted by a panel to determine if they have the quality and typicity of the region.

Many other wine regions around the world have not added tasting panels to approve the outgoing wines. Apart from possibly not having as much history making one style, they argue that placing that level of stricture on a wine region inhibits the freedom of growers to experiment, stopping cultural expression and limiting what consumers might be able to experience. Some critics might add that occasionally tasting panels are added to regions that don't even have that long a history, and are intended as a way of indicating that the history of that taste is timeless and traditional when, in reality, it might not be that old.

Is it really the case that wine regions with more restrictions about what can be grown are less innovative? The idea of innovation is broad and examples may be subtle, but one obvious example is the Super-Tuscan movement, where producers planted Bordelais varieties and bottled them under *vino da tavola*, or table wine, rather than their more specific regional place name, which they would not have been permitted to do. Some might argue that the fact that they were able to do it is sufficient evidence alone to prove that innovation is possible. After all, there is no rule stating that they cannot make changes, just that they cannot use the regional place name when they do so. Others might push back, suggesting that this might work for a few wealthy wineries with healthy marketing budgets, but that for most wineries, the incentive to maintain the place name and the practices that go with it practically discourages innovation.

Another example of innovation coming into conflict with regional rules is the case of wineries advocating for low-intervention techniques in South Africa, a country that includes a tier of more controlled wine rules. These wineries may choose to bottle their wines with noticeable levels of volatile acidity, which can smell of vinegar or nail polish remover. This practice risks regional tasting committees jettisoning a producer's wine from place-name status on the grounds that it is atypical for the region. Wine writer Jim Clarke has observed, "The committee has adapted to recognize them [low intervention wines], although perhaps not as quickly as the producers in question would like."[39]

Some could argue that removing these wines from the market is a justification of the system, not just to preserve a consistent style so consumers know what to expect, but to protect consumers against obvious flaws. Allowing wines that many would dislike into the market might harm the collective reputation of a given region, which could have real and damaging effects on the larger group, even if the change is intentional. Others would argue that sometimes what consumers demand does not line up with what a tasting panel wants, and by denying the public what they want, or at least delaying it, the region cannot respond to consumer demands. Region rule defenders warn that allowing for the loss of a collective taste identity should only be done at one's economic peril.

How quickly to change, what change to allow, and who gets to decide the change are some of the key questions. The larger question of enforcing stylistic unity may lead one to muse: If regional bodies need to restrict producers' choices to attain a sense of typicity, is this not a subtle acknowledgment that typicity of place does not wholly derive from terroir? Does this acknowledgment undermine the integrity of the promise of terroir, or does it allow for an even set of rules to allow for it to better be seen? Which side is more right and whether these two positions are mutually exclusive will likely be debated as long as wine is made.

Given the importance of how grapes are grown and wine is made, some regions have responded by creating rules that place the process of creating the wines more centrally in the explanation to consumers. Germany's historic categorization of wine by sugar in the grapes at harvest, or Rioja's tiers defined by time in barrel, let consumers know what type of wine they should expect, and this sort of system could be expanded globally with relative ease. Part of the reason this system perhaps hasn't gained as much traction as region-based wine designations is this ease of replicability. It's hard for a winery to create a marketing edge when any other winery can copy the high-end version of a product. And of course, many argue that site is more important.

* * *

Amidst all the complexity of rules, places, and tasting panels, it is important to be reminded that, in theory, the goal of wine regions and the rules within them is to provide clarity. A chief goal of the geographic indicator system is to provide transparency and clarity to consumers. By publicizing enological and viticultural restrictions and expanding the PDO system to more countries, its advocates reason that consumers would be more informed and therefore better off.

Critics contend that the differing sets of rules and the proliferation of regional place names would lead to overload of unhelpful information. This would, counterintuitively, confuse customers further, an outcome that the original French enemy of the AOC, the négociants, argued would happen.[40] For example,

Italy's DOCG is a distinct standard not shared by most European countries and although Spain's DOCa standard is similar, there are relatively few in Spain compared to the many in Italy, so comparison is less meaningful. The sheer number of regions to keep track of, and the various and complex rules, lead to what the scholar Timothy Josling, a Professor in the Food Research Institute at Stanford University, has called, "confused consumers with an overload of information of dubious value."[41]

Josling deepens his argument, suggesting that helping consumers was never the goal to begin with, noting, "It would be naïve to believe that GIs are solely for the protection of consumers. The keenest advocates of systems of GI registration are producer groups ... GIs confer some degree of market power, and the associated rents are the reward for gaining legal protection against competitors."[42]

Those pushing back on this argument might open with the idea that producers surely benefit, but they argue that those benefits are justified. They might also push back on the idea that regional regulations provide chaos and confusion because relative to a wine world with no rules and order, at least there is some attempt to create order out of capitalism.

* * *

Part of the reason these questions regarding regional wine rules are so vexing is because they get at how to technically codify some of the core questions of wine. How do we decide where one terroir ends and another begins, should we evaluate the quality between two terroirs, how much freedom to decide farming methodology and winemaking should be given to the individual and how much should be a collective decision – and is the government a capable and appropriate agent to make these decisions? By combining political science with how wine is made, it is no surprise that legal scholars have spent their lives on these questions. The centuries to come will be the testing ground to see if the regional rules converge or diverge, but they will be unlikely to stay the same forever.

3
The organic question

"In undertaking farming we undertake a responsibility covering the whole life cycle. We can break it or keep it whole. We have broken it, but there is yet time to mend it; perhaps only just in time."

Walter James, the fourth Lord Northbourne[1]

In the summer of 1920, a year after fleeing to Switzerland based on the rumor that he would be hunted as a war criminal for his role in the gas warfare of World War I,[2] Fritz Haber arrived in Copenhagen to be fêted as the winner of the Nobel Prize in Chemistry. Ascending to the stage to accept the prize, he reflected on the previously unimaginable feat of synthesizing ammonia mechanically, and later reflected, "Nitrogen bacteria teach us that Nature, with her sophisticated forms of the chemistry of living matter, still understands and utilizes methods which we do not as yet know how to imitate. Let it suffice that in the meantime improved nitrogen fertilization of the soil brings new nutritive riches to mankind and that the chemical industry comes to the aid of the farmer who, in the good earth, changes stones into bread."[3]

Haber was by no means the first chemist to modernize how plants were grown. The pace of agricultural research had quickened dramatically in the nineteenth century, as scientists sought to industrialize the field and delve deeper into plant nutrition. Justus Von Liebig, credited with helping to found organic chemistry in the nineteenth century, is cited as the father of the fertilizer industry and preached the importance of scientific plant nutrition from his buzzing university laboratory in Germany. This emphasis led to a mad dash for sources of fertilizer, most notably guano (the droppings of seabirds or bats) which contained nitrogen, phosphate, and potassium.

Pesticides and fungicides were also being developed, offering a promise of salvation from crop-destroying pathogens that could create hardship, famines, and death. Given these grim choices it is no surprise that farmers have adapted to using pesticides, but even then there were hints that this type of progress had its downsides. Prefacing an 1896 account of the burgeoning use of chemicals in agriculture, B. T. Galloway, the chief of the division of vegetable plant pathology at the United States Department of Agriculture, wrote, "So phenomenal has been the progress in this direction that we are sometimes led to think that we have gone forward too fast, for in our intense desire to make the work thoroughly practical we have in many cases merely skimmed the surface, overlooking some of the most important fundamental questions involved."[4]

Vintners, like other farmers, were swept up in this agricultural sea-change, some waiting for scientific recommendations, and others experimenting on their own. In the mid-nineteenth century, a German vintner reported dipping rags in an iron sulfate solution and having workers physically wash every vine[5] and in France it was reported that some vintners sprayed arsenic in their vineyards to terminate insects.[6] In the 1870s, to discourage theft of grapes, some Bordelais vintners painted their vines blue, hoping to make them look diseased and undesirable. This led to an unexpected discovery. The "paint" mixture of limewater and copper that they had applied had the unanticipated effect of protecting the vine against the recently discovered crop-eviscerating fungus downy mildew. The mixture came to be known as Bordeaux Mixture and was celebrated for its progress in helping vintners get a crop. "Confidence has thus again been restored where not more than ten years ago there prevailed the greatest anxiety regarding the future of the grape industry,"[7] wrote Ernest Lodeman, a Cornell University chemist and agricultural researcher in the 1890s.

While some celebrated the discoveries, progress and economic advancement brought about by innovations in plant nutrition and pesticides, others began questioning what dangers this new chemical era would usher in.

Albert Howard was a farmer's son born in Shropshire, Great Britain. After training in biological sciences at the University of Cambridge he was set to become one of the growing number of agricultural engineers that might increase farming efficiency. He moved to a newly minted research station in India in 1905, part of a wave of British scientists sent "to confer on the peoples of India all the advantages of Western scientific discovery."[8] In 1924, Maharaja Tukojirao Holkar III of the Indore State donated land for a new Institute of Plant Industry.[9] Though his initial mission was to research plant diseases and improve yields,[10] over the course of his 26 years in India, Howard and others began to question the direction agricultural science was quickly moving in.

Howard's line of advocacy challenged the zeitgeist of agricultural practice, demonizing the father of fertilizer, Justus Von Liebig, as "half a man" for his focus solely on science, without having practical knowledge of farming.[11] Howard referred to chemical fertilizer as "artificial manure,"[12] just as others of his generation referred to cars as horseless carriages. Ultimately he argued that it was possible to farm using cover crops, manure and nothing else.

Howard's thinking was informed by many other influences, including the holistic approach to plant pathology of his Cambridge Professor, Marshall Ward, contributions from fellow scientists at Indian research stations, the 1921 research findings of H. B. Hutchinson and E. H. Richards on composting, the collaboration and support from his botanist wife, Gabrielle, and the teachings of the Indian farmers who he called his "professors of agriculture."[13] Although Howard was influential, it is difficult to attribute organics to any one individual as there were a number of people who were vocal or instrumental in bringing about what is now called organic farming, including Lord Northbourne, Lady Eve Balfour, Ewald Könemann, Mina Hofstetter, and Jerome Rodale, to name a few.[14]

When organic viticulture was first started, the focus was on the type of fertilizer – natural or synthetic – applied to the plant. As the twentieth century went on, more advanced synthetic pesticides were invented and utilized to control insects, weeds, and fungal growth. Though chemical sprays had been used before the twentieth century, the volume shot up after World War II. In the agriculture of the United States, pesticide use skyrocketed from the sixties to the early eighties, though grapes accounted for a very small percentage of this.[15] Rachel Carson, in her 1962 book *Silent Spring*, warned about the use of the pesticide DDT, short for dichlorodiphenyltrichloroethane, which had been used in at least some vineyards as early as the 1940s and 1950s.[16, 17] The organic movement in the United States evolved to become a back-to-the-land ethic that resisted the rise of chemical use in agriculture. Vintners took notice of this broadening focus, with calls to ban all synthetic chemicals quickly following.

Although advances in chemical knowledge were progressing rapidly, the key themes of the organic question remained the same: traditional farming versus modernity, naturalness versus chemical synthesis, and how to measure success and failure in farming. Part of the reason the organic debate figures so prominently is because the impacts of global farming are so monumental. Agriculture is responsible for between a quarter to a third of all greenhouse gas emissions and takes up four out of every ten cubic feet of land on earth.[18] At the same time, increased efficiencies in farming have been able to create more food and lower prices. Although certainly not solving global hunger, this has gone a long way in giving the global population better access to food and varied sources of nutrition.

Though grape growing is a small slice of the agricultural pie, vineyards' share of the impact warrants the question of whether vintners should convert to organic practices. It was not always assumed that wine would feature prominently in the larger organic story. In the U.S.A., organic wine, in the modern, certified sense, began in the 1980s[19] when restaurants began featuring organic food[20] and certifications were on the rise.[21, 22] Surveys from 2019 show global vine acreage was 6.2 percent organic. As trends suggest this percentage is growing, the pace of vineyard-specific research has quickened, shedding new light on what effect this farming has on land and vines. For many in the industry, despite its relatively recent arrival, organic certification represents the best hope for responsible farming.

* * *

Before jumping into the fray to contend with the legion of arguments for and against organic winegrowing, we need to ask a simple, yet surprisingly complex question. What is organic wine? The rules of organic farming were initially the purview of the organic movement, but after governments began passing laws to sanction or govern organic farming, the creation and interpretation of the rules fell to government departments, board appointees, and sometimes judges. An ostensibly straightforward statement, like, "I'm for organic viticulture" could draw the questions "Which country's definition?" or "Are you still in favor of it after the controversial changes at last year's meeting?"

The United States Department of Agriculture, tasked by Congress with developing organic regulation in 1990, struggled with the task throughout the next decade. Upon the publication of its first attempt at a set of rules, the USDA received more public comments than any other regulation in the department's history going back to its founding by the pen of President Abraham Lincoln in 1862.[23] The result of this arduous public debate was a preference for natural farm inputs, though with an important caveat. The USDA permitted a list of approved synthetics,[24] in which exceptions were made for materials that were judged absolutely necessary or where a natural means of production is impractical.²⁵ For example, Polyoxin D zinc salt is permitted in part due to the limitations of organic fungicides despite strong opposition when it was approved.²⁶ Sulfur, a natural element, is categorized as a permitted synthetic in the United States because it is commonly a by-product of petroleum refineries.²⁷ There is some irony that a petroleum by-product is one of the most commonly used sprays in a naturally-inclined system of farming. On the other hand, products like arsenic were banned due to their toxicity despite being 100 percent natural.²⁸

Across the pond, the European Union's organic rules betray disagreement with certain American conclusions, illustrating how different regulatory regimes can disagree on the principles of organics. In 2012, Europe added organic rules for wine processing in addition to farming, capping sulfur levels in wine – lower than for non-organic European wines²⁹ but higher than the zero-tolerance organic standard of the United States.³⁰ This is why some organic European wines must be relabeled as "wine made with organic grapes" for sale in the United States.³¹ It is worth noting that the European Union and the United States have perhaps more significant policy disagreements on issues unrelated to wine, for example where the EU prohibits Concentrated Animal Feeding Operations (CAFOs) and hydroponics, the United States has allowed these practices under organics.³² Though these and other differences continue throughout the world of organics, there has been significant negotiation work to harmonize organic rules to allow for international trade of these goods, ensuring that the overlying principles are similar if not almost identical.³³

The sulfur difference between the United States and Europe is perhaps the most notable and widely cited organic distinction in wine, but it illustrates that for countries that have accepted and adopted organic rules, there is still a thriving debate about what organics should be. Knowing when to limit natural products that ongoing research may reveal to be harmful, as in the cases of arsenic and copper, is a question organic regulators have had to wrestle with. Another question has been raised by the development of new biopesticides that can play at the boundaries of how to define natural. The case of Polyoxin D zinc salt is an example of a difficult decision in which the U.S. narrowly allowed it but the EU did not.

Scott Rice, who has served on both the National Organics Standard Board (NOSB) and the Organic Materials Review Institute (OMRI), is the regulatory director of the Organic Trade Association, a membership association that lobbies Washington D.C. for organic interests. He acknowledges the difficulty for people on those boards in interpreting organic principles for individual products at the margin. "You often operate in a lot of gray as much as it's a black and white regulation," he says.[34] The determination of whether a farming additive is approved hinges on the degree to which it has been chemically processed, and as Rice acknowledges, making that determination can be difficult: "It's a point of conversation that has been rather heated over the years."[35]

Despite instances of disagreement, regulators around the world agree on the core organic fundamentals. After reviewing the organic regulatory texts of various governments, one group of researchers concluded, "Despite the broader definitions used in preambles of organic regulatory texts, organic regulations are, in practice, defining organic agriculture as a chemical-free management system, based on avoiding synthetic inputs, and relying on natural substances instead."[36, 37]

* * *

One of the wine researchers who has reviewed the agricultural science literature on organic viticulture is Ronald Jackson, a native of Canada and author of one of the most popular enology textbooks, *Wine Science: Principles and Applications*. At six pounds and 11 ounces (around 3 kilos), the fifth edition weighs about the same as a newborn baby. With topics ranging from the molecular structures of proanthocyanidin oligomers to the hydrostatic gradient of the xylem, the book is a great resource for anyone who thinks they know everything about wine and is in need of being humbled.

Jackson shows no sign of slowing down. The fifth and most recent edition of *Wine Science* was published in 2020, but given the pace of research on organic wine, Jackson readily acknowledges that even in a few short years, "A lot has changed since then."[38] In the beginning of organics, many were skeptical of a movement caricatured as back-to-the land types wearing tie-dye and toting peace signs, but with the ascendancy of organic studies to universities, the movement went on to gain scientific and popular respectability.

Surrounded by books and microscopes, Jackson muses, "The more I've looked into organic viticulture, the more I've realized that there is no such thing as simple organic viticulture."[39] Putting aside the differing ways countries have defined and regulated organics, there are a plethora of approaches to practicing organic viticulture, and just as crucially, a plethora of approaches to managing vines non-organically.

The most extreme possible counterpoint to organic vinegrowing is to use all the most dangerous and controversial pesticides with reckless abandon, and overwork the soil until it resembles moon dust. In this scenario, any scientific study comparing the results would be able to easily show the differences. A more moderated position would be to farm organically except once in three years apply a marginally processed version of potassium that is more plant assimilable. There is a chasm between these two farming approaches, which illustrates the difficulty in finding a singular form of "conventional" farming to scientifically compare to organics.

Similarly, when examining organic farming, we must ask: Was a cover crop grown? If so, what type, and was it tilled in or not? Were conditions particularly challenging or favorable for the period being studied? For example, some years with more rain or humidity can cause more mildew growth compared to dry years, so the farming challenges faced will be radically different. There are many variables that make black-and-white comparisons of organic and non-organic farming very difficult, meaning that the general public should be skeptical of any bold conclusions drawn from one year of data.

A French research team pointed out that in one long-term study, it took between seven and eleven years before they could measure differences between the organic and non-organic farming system.[40] And even if the time is taken to work through a comparison, due to the different disease pressures around the world, using data and know-how from southern France and applying it to vines in West Australia could work out, or it could result in viticultural malpractice. With that clarified, there has been fascinating and surprising quality research that can help determine the impacts of these distinct approaches to vineyards.

* * *

Haroula Spinthiropoulou, a star winemaker from Greece, is on Team Organic. "I am convinced that organic cultivation creates a healthier soil over time," she writes.[41] When organic growers refer to healthy soils they are often referencing soils with a decent reserve of organic matter which is measured as the percentage of soil made up of animal, plant, and bacterial detritus.[42] To achieve these ends, organic growers apply compost and other organic fertility to soil, eschewing synthetic fertilizers. Before jumping into pesticides or anything else, this question of whether to limit sources of fertility is the beginning of the debate.

John Reganold, an agricultural research professor at Washington State University, has said that over a lifetime of visiting hundreds – possibly thousands – of farms he observes that one thing unites the organic growers, "I have never not been shown the soil … Every time I go out – 'Hey, John, I got to show you this. Look at all these earthworms here. Look at my structure. Look how black this is. Look at the roots. Look at this!' I've never once ever been shown the soil on a conventional farm."[43]

One of the reasons these farmers value organic matter is because it reduces soil erosion and runoff, allows water to percolate down to roots more easily, increases microbial diversity and acts as a reserve for nutrients that can be used by the vine.[44] It is worth pointing out that for grapevines, it is generally agreed that too much nutrition is not good for quality vines, but given the difficulty and expense of achieving high nutrition through compost and other organic fertilizers, its defenders would argue that too much organic compost will never be a quality concern.

One meta-study of various farms (not just vineyards) reported that organic matter was consistently higher on organic plots of land. Even when non-organic sites added higher rates of manure compared to their organic counterparts, soil organic matter was not significantly different,[45] suggesting that amendment addition was not the only important factor in play and that organic growers were at an advantage.

Not only do organic vineyards tend to have more organic matter, but also there are other microbial differences in the soil. In 1885 Albert Bernhard Frank discovered that plant roots were covered in a mycorrhizal network.[46] In this symbiotic relationship, the plant receives nutrients from a fungus in exchange for sugars. A year later, Hermann Hellriegel and Hermann Wilfahrt made an equally groundbreaking discovery, revealing that some bacteria can "fix" nitrogen, converting it into a form that makes it available to plants.[47] Previously, researchers had been guessing that the chemical make-up of the soil was all that mattered to plants, but after these discoveries many began to wonder if soil quality might have a significant role to play.

Almost a century and a half later, the preponderance of evidence indicates that on average organic vineyards have more mycorrhizal life than their conventional counterparts.[48, 49] As Lauren Hale, a USDA soil microbiologist, observes, "Many plants allocate more resources to beneficial microbial symbionts, such as arbuscular mycorrhizal fungi, in response to a nutrient deficit or stress. So, in soils with high mineral fertilizer inputs there is less need for symbionts and thus less selective pressure for the plant to recruit and promote root colonization by mycorrhizal fungi."[50]

It is unsurprising then that organic soils on average have more mycorrhizal networks.

Given the litany of benefits and the evidence that organics gets the job done, one might rightly ask why every vintner doesn't worship at the altar of organic fertilizer, whether that be compost or dry fish meal. But there is a reason why 96.7 percent of wine is not organic.[51] Robert Paarlberg, a scholar at Harvard's Kennedy School, has researched food politics extensively and is an organic skeptic. "What's the purpose of the soil? Is it to earn our respect for some of its soil-ness, or is it to make the production of abundant and nutritious food affordable?"[52] He points out that some of the original advocates of organic farming were privileged and landed to begin with, and is critical of the idea that organic sources of nutrition are better than their synthetic counterparts. He finds the idea that organic agriculture can scale up dubious at best: "Currently, large organic farms out in California get their manure from the livestock industry. Feedlots. Do you like feedlots? Is that your vision of a circular economy – returning manure to the soil through an industrial CAFO system? You know, there are limits to the scale at which you can produce food using pre-industrial, soil fertility products."[53]

Though Paarlberg's critique is focused on agriculture as a whole, organic vineyards are implicated in his criticism. Just like any plant, vineyards need nitrogen, phosphorus, potassium, and a series of micronutrients, and synthetic fertilizers do a good job of providing them. In fact, they were engineered specifically to be assimilable to plants, whereas organic fertilizers don't have the same impact pound for pound, which is one of the reasons it can be more expensive. Some argue that organic fertilizers are not always uniform in nutrition content, which could result in some vines getting less nutrients than desired. Also, due to the time it takes for the organic fertilizer to be broken down and become plant assimilable, and due to the time windows that vines need to uptake particular nutrients, it is more difficult to get the timing right and succeed in farming.[54] With synthetic fertilizer, you measure a deficiency and fix it. The grapevine responds immediately. Organic compost takes longer.

The cautionary tale that anti-organic advocates point to is Sri Lanka, whose government banned the import of synthetic fertilizers. This caused food prices to skyrocket, leading to protests in the street and a hasty reversal of policy.[55] If the sustainable farming solution isn't sustainable at scale, is it sustainable to begin with? Organic advocates can respond, arguing that the policy shift was too sudden, not giving farmers enough training to get ready for a different way to manage crops. Other governments have not given up on the organic dream. The EU set a plan in 2021 to make 25 percent of its farming land organic by 2030 and in California there is a goal to be 20 percent organic by 2045.[56, 57]

Whereas in general farming, maximizing crop is usually desired, in wine this is where the organic debate takes a left turn. Though the majority of wine in the world is affordable, and issues of yield matter, once the critic turns their attention to fine wine, the question of farming is different. If the sole interest of the vintner is quality, then they can argue that there is no need to answer theoretical questions about whether the entire world of agriculture needs to adopt organics – they just need to defend its use on their turf. And what's more, they can argue that better wine quality is achieved with low yields on rocky, nutrient-poor ground. Indeed, some of the most celebrated vineyards in the world are on such ground. If an organic compost system can work in the context of fine wine, why – they might ask – is it necessary to spend the money on synthetics?

The response from non-organic vintners would be not that synthetic forms of nitrogen or potassium don't have to be abused, in fact, the applications can be measured better. The fact that most cheap wine comes from synthetic fertilizer does not mean that it has to be misapplied by an intelligent vigneron who measures her vines to determine the minimum necessary nutrition needed. And what's more, if non-organic farmers are convinced of the benefits of compost and cover crop, as many of them are, they can still apply it to gain the benefits – farming in the exact way that most organic vintners do – but they also have the freedom to give their plants a nutrient if the vine is weak in a particular micronutrient and does not seem to be getting it from the organic fertilizer.

In comparing these methods, one way of determining soil health is the humble earthworm. By burrowing and excreting in the soil, these soil denizens can increase the water retention of vineyard land by four to ten times,[58] a quality particularly desirable in drier climates. Organic practitioners are quick to reach for earthworms as yet another feather in their farming caps, given that worm-friendly practices like compost applications and cover crops are mainstays of organic practice and research from the 1990s has showed greater earthworm activity in organic plots.[59, 60]

However, a long-term study in the south of France comparing different farming systems made a surprising discovery. There was in fact less earthworm activity in organic vineyard sites.[61] It's not immediately clear why, but apart from built-up levels of copper, one theory is that the tillage often accompanying organic vineyards to increase fertility might be responsible.[62] After pointing out some of the benefits of organics, the study's authors ended with a pessimistic conclusion: "Our study highlights the difficulty to show the benefits of organic farming on global soil quality in this particular pedoclimatic area and set of farming practices."[63] Given that organic practitioners have a wide variety of views on cover crops and how frequently tillage is needed, and some sites might need more or less copper than others, we can expect the worm debate to wriggle on.

Another contested point underneath the umbrella of fertilizer choice is the extent to which runoff and pollution is possible. Agricultural runoff into lakes and streams creates algal-infested dead zones that kill fish.[64, 65] Some claim that runoff is most likely when using synthetic fertilizer, in large part because of the on-average better soil structure on organic farms that can reduce runoff.[66] They claim there are fewer confusing synthetic chemicals that might wash away and the type of people who choose to become organic growers are likely to care more about environmental issues and would therefore manage the issue better. Some research in non-vineyard sites found less nitrate leaching in organic sites compared to non-organic sites.[67]

Others claim that heavy metal leaching and other runoff can come from organic sources, too.[68, 69] Using organic forms of fertilizer is not a panacea that magically eliminates the risk of fertilizer runoff, these critics argue,[70] and even in organics, caution must be taken. Measuring the differences and likelihood of possible runoff in vineyards around the world in differing slopes and conditions is difficult to do at scale.

Though most of the arguments in the organic soil deliberation are practical, the debate tends to circle back to the unquantifiable value placed on the natural world. Howard, in an almost spiritual exhortation, writes, "Chemicals can never be a substitute for humus because Nature has ordained that the soil must live and the mycorrhizal association must be an essential link in plant nutrition."[71] Though the ongoing and future scientific research on soil health will ultimately provide the most value in weighing and accounting for the current set of arguments, invoking Nature with a capital N is a telling allusion to the powerful idea behind the movement. For some, these more ephemeral and hard-to-measure values are central. Especially for wine, maximizing naturalness in the course of making wine is desired in its own right by many, even if it is imperfectly natural. This impractical element that can frustrate its critics is exactly what its advocates celebrate.

* * *

Though organics has been defined as one singular farming approach, it can be conceptualized as having two sides: the nutritional side – the debate on whether fertilizers should be natural or not – and the second aspect, that of pesticides. This took a number of decades to take prominence within the organic movement. As William Lockeretz, who wrote and edited a history of organics, noted, "Organic farming's goals regarding agricultural and social politics changed from preservation of rural life during the 1950s and 1960s to environmental protection during the 1980s and 1990s."[72] As the movement wrestled with what its goals should be, it attempted to balance tensions over the degree to which it should be results oriented (measuring the residual pesticides in the product) or values oriented (focusing on natural inputs regardless of outcome).

Dr. Karen Morrison represents the state of California's approach to agrochemical regulation. She graduated with distinction and a Bachelor of Science degree in chemistry from Harvey Mudd College, and went on to get a PhD in organic chemistry from the University of Illinois Urbana-Champaign. After serving as the Senior Environmental Scientist for CalRecycle, Morrison began work at the California Department of Pesticide Regulation (DPR), quickly moving up to become the Chief Deputy Director and Science Advisor, a position she assumed in 2022.

In contrast to the organic standards board, which accounts for the level of naturalness or processing of a farm input when considering whether to approve it for use, Morrison explains the view of the State of California: "We review all pesticides pretty much using the same set of standards. Just because something originated from a biological system does not inherently make it safe."[73] Some might critique organics on this point, arguing that its puritanical focus on naturalness is less about safety and more a showcase of the naturalness fallacy in action.

Organic advocates would be quick to defend their theory of how to review new pesticides. In creating their own pesticide residue tolerances at levels lower than those deemed safe by government scientists, the implicit claim by some in the movement is that governments are too lax in their permissiveness and enforcement of synthetic chemicals, so an overly cautious approach is preferable. Governments face pressure from lobbyists to approve chemicals convenient to industry, given the complexity of chemical interactions in the environment they could make errors, and sometimes administrations show a disregard for environmental concerns, which could undermine regulatory safeguards. Under this view, organic advocates are being extra cautious, but rational.

It is difficult to estimate what portion of organic wine producers use this as their reason for being organic, but for some, the idea that no synthetic pesticide is good, even in infinitesimal parts-per-billion levels, is central to their justification. There are likely differences in how organic vintners view chemical residues from natural toxins or approved synthetics, such as sulfur and calcium hydroxide, though because this distinction is well within the weeds of the topic, it does not get much public discourse, at least within the world of wine.

As for the argument that organic rules are more focused on naturalness than safety, organic advocates can reply saying that human safety is a base barrier to clear and only then do they go on to assess naturalness. For example, a compound deemed safe but not natural would be unlikely to be approved under organics, whereas a compound that is natural but not safe, like tobacco dust, would never be approved. Tobacco dust was formerly used in viticulture – in 1913 the *New York Times* published a story entitled *Vineyards Seek Nicotine*, reporting "It is used for spraying grapevines and fruit trees almost everywhere in France, as it has been found particularly efficacious as an insecticide."[74] (The newspaper went on to note that due to low supply of nicotine at this time, French vignerons were having to resort to "less desirable substances.") It is worth noting that in the modern era natural but unsafe substances would in theory be banned in non-organic farming as well by most governments, and the classic examples of organically banned natural substances – tobacco dust and arsenic – have been banned or limited by general farming regulations as well.

There has been research on the modern-day effect of pesticide drift too. One 2019 study coming out of France showed a link between ethylenethiourea, which can be used as a spray, and rhinitis in children[75] which involves hay fever like symptoms.[76]

Certainly, synthetic pesticides often have a higher toxicity than their organic counterparts, and some argue this risk should lead the consumer to prefer organics.

Critics of organics argue that many of these claims are unfounded. If the reason for doubt in the system is a lack of trust in governments, they can argue that the same argument would work against organics as well since the same governments ultimately oversee organic legislation and regulation. Naturally derived plant sprays can also be dangerous, and the same safety standards should apply to them without pretending that the same challenges don't apply. And given the safety measures taken by governments on all agriculture, not to mention the vineyard teams themselves, it can be argued that the risks of synthetic chemicals are exaggerated by people with a profit incentive linked to the success of the organic brand or people who instinctively fear or don't understand how chemistry works.

Some vintners who chose to remain anonymous pointed out that sulfur sprays, as used by organic and non-organic growers alike, are not healthy to ingest either. Some organic advocates might suggest their wines have lower pesticide residues, but critics can point out that, if there is actually a compound that is demonstrably proving harm to a community, the best form of public advocacy would not be to drink organic wines, but to advocate that all wines change so as to avoid a two-tiered system of health.

The question still stands of why the level of processing of a product should play any role at all in deciding its suitability for organic farming, as opposed to judging all inputs solely based on safety and efficacy. Linley Dixon, who holds a PhD in plant pathology, is the leader of the Real Organic Project, an add-on certification to USDA Organics in the United States that was formed after the USDA allowed hydroponics and reduced stringency on dairy operations. As someone who both believes in the values behind organics and who has thought deeply about to what degree the U.S. government's interpretation of those values is in keeping with the spirit of organics, she is well qualified to opine on these issues. She pushes back on the assumption behind the question, that organic regulation can be boiled down to its inputs. "They try to just say, look at how stupid they are. They're trying to say that this naturally occurring compound is different from the synthetically occurring compound. It's not about that. It's taking a step back and seeing the system as a whole."[77]

So, the critique of organic's approach to chemicals is that it relies on the naturalist fallacy in deciding fertilizer, and the defense is to suggest that this view is missing the forest for the trees. Limiting their inputs forces growers to think about a farm or a vineyard less like a doctor giving medicine to a patient and more like a nutritionist preventing sickness through holistic diet and living. From this perspective, the grape grower with particularly pernicious weeds ought to work on their fertility and the whole ecosystem – they need to think broader and more creatively rather than about their spray program, and this way of thinking makes them a better farmer.

One grape grower, who has worked with organic and non-organic vineyards and chose to remain anonymous to be able to speak openly, is skeptical that organic growers always see more holistically than non-organic growers. "I think we're always creative whether you're an organic farmer or not." Though non-organic growers certainly claim to see grape farming systems as holistically as their counterparts, organic growers can respond by suggesting that the inability to be able to turn to a pesticide means organic vintners *need* to think more broadly and preventatively. If they don't have a strong synthetic treatment for a disease, then finding a way to prevent it is not a convenience, it is necessary. This mental switch is part of the focus on holistic systems.

Dixon expands on her argument by invoking the precautionary principle. She recounts the story of the U.S. government approving sewage sludge as a form of manure in the 1970s, and decades later discovering that the cows that grazed on this land produce milk containing forever chemicals, probably due to what had been dumped down toilets. Organic farmers had resisted this approach without necessarily knowing why, according to Dixon, and she argues this type of skepticism and intuition can pay off. This is the principle that undergirds naturalness in inputs over new synthetic compounds. "We are going to put our money in the systems that evolved over hundreds of millions of years," Dixon says.[78]

The underlying question is whether a default preference for naturalness in farming inputs is a necessary starting point for a holistic mindset for the precautionary principle to work. The precautionary principle could be better served by rigorous testing for harms, low legal residue levels, and more research to see how various compounds interact with one another. Organic critics can argue that existing regulations have already been created in response to these exact same concerns and are already very rigorous in defending the environment and the consumer. As DPR Director Karen Morrison observes, "I think it's true in a lot of areas around environmental regulation in general, it's just that if it's working well, people tend to not talk about it."[79] After all, does having a synthetic cleaning spray in one's kitchen stop one from thinking holistically or safely?

Regardless of the individual decisions on particular pesticides, another way of measuring the worth of organics, in viticulture or in general, is whether the movement has succeeded in changing farming for the better. Paul Thompson, a philosopher who spent his academic career looking at agriculture, notes of organics: "It has reduced the toxic load on the environment. Perhaps not as much as hoped, or enough to achieve deep significance, but it's not nothing, and it's given consumers an alternative."[80]

While some agree with this assessment, others can question whether organic farming has been the main cause of pesticide reduction. Forces apart from organics have led to reductions in pesticide use. Robert Paarlberg points out that Rachel Carson, whose publication of *Silent Spring* was enormously influential in the regulatory crackdown on synthetic chemicals, never went all the way and said there should be none – she just wanted the incontestably toxic ones like DDT to go and others to be thoughtfully and prudently regulated.[81] It is difficult to determine exactly which social forces caused the reduction of pesticides and that historical question is likely to be contested.

Though the conversation about pesticides revolves around synthesis, this is often a proxy conversation for the real issue at hand: toxicity. The very reason that many synthetic pesticides and herbicides are used over their organic counterparts is because of their strength, and therein lies the potential risk. Part of the trouble with deciding what is toxic is that anything can be harmful to organisms (human or otherwise) depending on the amount. Paracelsus, a Swiss-born Renaissance man who played a key role in advancing thought in medicine, observed as early as the sixteenth century, "What is there that is not poison? All things are poison and nothing is without poison. Solely the dose determines that a thing is not a poison."[82] It is by puzzling over these quandaries that he came to be known as the father of toxicology, and the principles he discussed are still key questions when wrestling with how to conceptualize organic farming.

After any spray hits a vine, the question becomes what happens when or if it gets into the soil. In many cases, repeated toxic sprays can turn what was once a complex humus high in organic matter into something more akin to moon dust, with no sign of a blade of grass. It is hard to imagine much life in the soil when it is treated this way. Dr. Johanna Döring, the Chair of Organic Viticulture at Geisenheim University, the best-known winemaking school in Germany, notes that understanding how pesticides leach into soil is easier said than done. "This is a very difficult topic. We have been measuring residues of plant protection agents on grapes, but as soon as they are degraded or metabolized in the soil, it is very difficult or almost impossible to trace them."[83] This lack of clarity means there is still some mystery left as to what effect some common herbicides can have on the soil.

Justine Vanden Heuvel, a horticultural professor within Cornell's enology school, observes that synthetic sprays are not the only chemicals that can affect the soil. "I think on the whole, in the discussion about organics, people overlook the toxicity of copper."[84] A 2020 paper found that an organically managed plot had higher levels of copper in the soil compared to the conventional counterpart. Research is beginning to show that copper, when above certain limits, damages soil fertility and possibly harms mycorrhizae.[85, 86] The European Commission's modification of organic standards to 4 kilograms per hectare per year is a tacit acknowledgment of the harms that had been caused, with research showing that the new legal threshold is low enough to keep the biological life in soils functioning well.[87] As copper is one of the few tools organic growers have in their kit, the question will be how to balance the needs of vintners to fight fungal infections while preserving soil life.

Another factor weighing on the debate is soil compaction. Very compact soils can limit water and nutrients available to the vine.[88] One of the repercussions of organic farming, critics contend, is that by using less toxic sprays, the number of tractor passes to get the job done has to go up.[89, 90] If those extra sprays are applied via a tractor, then in theory the soil should be compacted more on average. This has been borne out in some research and is one of the criticisms sometimes leveled at organic vineyards.[91] However, one of the few holistic studies conducted on this topic found that there was not a significant difference in soil compaction, and the authors hypothesized that the cover crop in the organic vineyard was able to help reverse compaction via its root system.[92] In the University of Geisenheim research on soil compaction that Dr. Döring ran, she found that the organic site had less compaction despite needing two more tractor passes than the control, and also suspects that root activity played a role in explaining this. More research will undoubtedly come out in different viticultural regions and with different soil conditions, and more studies could be done comparing organic sites that might need more passes or with non-organic sites that use cover crops.

Moving on from the soil, many organic vintners contend that their vineyards are more beneficial for the surrounding ecosystem, allowing native plants and animals to thrive around and even within the vineyard, with benefits like greater species diversity and a better environment for fauna. Sound research demonstrates that on average biodiversity is higher on and around an organic farm.[93, 94] One team examining vineyards near Bordeaux concluded that although there was not enough evidence of difference in bird population in organics versus conventional farming, there were more spiders in organic vineyards,[95] a finding buttressed by similar conclusions in a British study from 2024.[96] And then there is the fairly unsurprising finding that organic vineyards tend to have more weed diversity as well.[97]

In the quarter century leading up to 2017, scientists estimate that insect populations have declined 75 percent. Though all the causes remain uncertain, an accusatory finger can be directed at farmers who spray toxic pesticides.[98, 99] It is not much of a leap to suggest that reducing the toxic chemicals in vineyards might be a good goal to have. Pesticides are generally regulated with the assumption that they are used as instructed, but a skeptic might have a hard time imagining that every vintner everywhere is using pesticides without error, exactly in the way the instructions direct.

There is a critique of this view. One viticulturist who wanted to remain anonymous, when presented with evidence that the local weed and arthropod ecology might be weaker because of their vineyard practices, responded that not all weeds and insects are beneficial or desirable. Using a metric of total quantity might not be helpful because in their region, some insects are vectors for disease that could destroy vineyards entirely or cause other chaos. These critics contend that more ecological diversity is great until part of that diversity tries to kill you or your livelihood.

"Fuckin' mealybugs are terrible," said another grower who chose to remain anonymous, explaining why their flirtation with organic practices was foiled. Mealybugs – tiny, scaly insects resembling prehistoric creatures from the Mariana Trench – are a disease vector that feeds on the vascular tissue (phloem) of the vine. This grower claimed to want to be organic, but after hitting the vineyard with many rounds of organic sprays to no avail, they turned to the greater arsenal of synthetic chemicals to get the job done.

Apart from the practical realities of farming, critics would point out that not all research suggests that organic viticulture provides superior environmental results. A research team from France's National Research Institute for Agriculture, Food and Environment (INRAE) concluded there is "an overall neutral effect of organic farming on biodiversity conservation."[100] This view points to the fact that some practices that help ecology, like integrated pest management, cover crops, and responsible management of spray programs, might be able to achieve environmental benefits without farmers having to resort to purity tests for their farming inputs. Dr. Karen Morrison, in attempting to explain the choice of using synthetic sprays, makes an analogy: "I use this example for people a lot. You have a spider in your house. You're going to make different decisions about how you manage a spider. For example, what if it's a single spider, it's a family of spiders, or it's the thirtieth that you've seen this week?"[101]

Mike Tyson said that everybody has a plan until they get punched in the face. For Glenn McGourty, that punch in the face came in the form of two weeds in his vineyard: fluvellin and Bermuda grass. McGourty spent much of his career as a University of California Plant Science Advisor, advising wine growers on vineyard management, and he specialized in organic wine grapes, writing a book on the topic to help vintners learn how to go organic. With these weeds, which can significantly stunt vine growth, he resorted to a synthetic herbicide. He found mechanical removal was too expensive and impractical. Another grower may have taken a different approach, but the trade-offs make it a difficult choice either way.

McGourty made that decision aware of the larger environmental concerns weighing in the balance, and is concerned about the long-term risks posed by some particularly strong sprays like pre-emergents more generally or paraquat or glyphosate more specifically. He explains the long-term consequences of systematically spraying a toxin, in this case glyphosate: "What happens if you're doing Roundup ready everything is that you're creating a huge weed problem because sooner or later everything seems to get resistance," he observes.[102] This potential doom loop, where stronger and stronger sprays lead to more resilient super weeds, not to mention insects, might lead to an uncharted and dangerous future.

Still, there is a question of whether organics is the best solution to these challenges. Part of the critique of organic farming is that it is so focused on toxicity and synthesis that it loses track of greater environmental goals. A 2017 analysis of different laws on organics summarized the following:

Our analysis supports the frequent criticism that the codification of organic practices has led to a reductionist perspective of organic agriculture, focused on avoidance of synthetic inputs. The prohibition of synthetic inputs does not, by itself, constitute more environmental friendly management, or represent a sufficient condition for sustainability, and may not even be a necessary one."[103]

Those skeptical of organic farming can argue that as long as the toxin in question is used safely, whether it be an organic sulfur spray or something stronger, this is what matters. They also point out that because of its focus on synthetic chemistry, organics forgoes other important environmental goals. The global organic regulatory report goes on:

Few of the regulations, for example, discuss water conservation, and none require specific irrigation practices, even though agriculture is the largest user of freshwater worldwide, and increasing water use efficiency is a major concern for sustainable agriculture. Only the Australian and Mexican regulations have detailed discussions of water management, for example requiring farmers to conserve water and to use local water resources without impacting flora and fauna.[104]

For organic advocates, many of whom share the concern about water conservation and efficacy of environmental impact, these critiques are not good reasons to disregard organics. On the water issue they can point to the water-retaining qualities of good soil structure. That it is not a panacea solving every environmental problem is not a reason to reject it, particularly when it is compared to non-organic practices.

Within organics, some vintners make more or less bold claims about ecological benefits, but Ria D'Aversa, who teaches viticulture at Cornell University and who also farms her own vineyard, summarizes the view of many sanguine organic growers: "I still believe though it is our ultimate job to care for the soil and our resources and organic does provide that a little bit more even though we're still putting out sulfur and heavy metals."[105]

Still, some organic vintners argue that their farming choices are not only limited to ecological effects, but can affect greenhouse gases as well. They contend that organic vineyards are less damaging because they better sequester carbon and because they don't depend on synthetic substances created through energy-intensive processes that may release additional pollutants and carbon dioxide into the atmosphere.[106] How can a type of farming be sustainable if it derives its inputs as by-products of the fossil fuel industry? Critics contest whether these impacts are as significant as suggested and some even argue that organics involves more manure, and thus more methane, which is a more harmful greenhouse gas,[107] and that the extra human labor and tractor passes create more emissions.[108]

A related question is how much yield an organic vineyard can deliver in contrast to one farmed without the restrictions of organics. Though some do claim that the yields of organics are the same as conventional, the academic perspective here is overwhelming: on average, organic vineyards produce a lower yield.[109] This may not be true in every climate and every year, and there are arguments for increased quality with lower yields, but on average it is the case. This is in part because copper and sulfur, the two primary weapons in the organic viticulturist's arsenal against fungal pathogens, act as protectants, whereas some synthetic options can more effectively fight mold and preserve grape tonnage.[110] Though in cases where quality producers are aiming for low yields to begin with, the yield gap between organic and non-organic shrank considerably,[111] so in context the organic difference may be less impactful for high-end wines.

This opens up a classic debate in ecology – is it best to farm less intensively to limit the potential damage brought about by this farming approach, or is it best to maximize yield on a smaller area of land so that more space can be preserved for nature? The anti-organic critique suggests that any attempt to mimic the semblance of a natural ecosystem is an act of hubris and will fall supremely short of an actual natural ecosystem. Thus, if organic farming is to take up a greater share of farming, given its average lower yields, it will eventually impinge on ecology and ultimately bring about more harmful effects.[112, 113, 114] Organic vintners can respond to suggest that they are such a small percentage of global agriculture that the effects are small, and that general land use regulations can prohibit vines going in ecologically sensitive areas.

Whether organic viticulture has the potential to expand rests on the question of how viable it is in different climates around the world and whether it is economical to do so. The expenses of organic farming vary widely by practice and circumstance. Joseph Brinkley, Director of Regenerative Organic Development at Bonterra Winery in California, and chair of the Organic Trade Association's newly formed Wine Council, says "I'm not sure if it's even possible, honestly, to farm *Vitis vinifera* organically on the east coast. I do think that this idea of context really, really does matter."[115] Though difficult to generalize for this reason, it's been estimated that organic winegrowing costs between 7 and 90 percent more than non-organic practices, though some research indicates in some instances organic farming can be more cost effective, making the margins fairly similar to conventional grapes on average.[116, 117]

Ria D'Aversa, of Cornell, emphasizes how financial circumstances can sometimes play a role. "I noticed that in a lot of vineyards that are certified organic or biodynamic, they are able to solve some issues because they do tend to have a little bit more financial advantage. You know, I think some people go toward synthetics not because that's what they've always done for 50 years, but they are also saying, well, that's what I can afford."[118] It may be difficult to ask a grower to go organic when there is no guarantee they'll be able to sell a good quantity of grapes at a competitive price, and for that same reason it is hard to be critical of a grower for not being organic if you don't know the challenges that their climate and their market are posing.

Though many consumers respond positively to organic wines, it's difficult to estimate if that goodwill would translate into consumers paying higher prices if the share of organic wine goes up. This may work in some regions or for some producers, but not all. And if one region can keep the cost of organic low and another region struggles, what obligation does the customer have to pay more for the wine from the difficult region? One 2017 paper out of Harvard Business School called organic wine a "case study in failed category creation." It also observed that it was a more popular category in cities and in northwestern Europe, noting that at the time, organic wine was more popular by volume in Sweden than the United States, despite Sweden's population being less than three percent of the U.S. population.[119] It is difficult to predict how the changing narrative about environmental stewardship will or will not change consumers' willingness to support this farming, and that in turn will affect whether this type of viticulture is economically sustainable.

One way that the organic wine industry could grow sustainably is if the promise to consumers was that organic wine was not only environmentally more friendly, but more delicious as well. This is arguably a more persuasive appeal to customers than pointing to the diminution of arthropods in non-organic vineyards. Some organic vintners have argued that due to the lower toxicity of sprays, the grapevine has more stressors and is forced to adapt, and that good tasters can discern the quality difference, despite it being hard to measure scientifically.[120] One research team has gone through the blind-tasting scores of wines from leading publications and confirmed that eco-certified wines, on average, get about 4.1 more points on a scaled 100-point metric than their non-certified counterparts.[121] Since this study is correlative and not causal, it's unclear if wineries that go organic improve their wines or if wineries already associated with quality choose to augment their marketing with eco-certifications.

One meta-analysis reported that organic wines might have more oxidative notes due to the lower average use of sulfur dioxide.[122] Despite some analysis showing that some compounds, such as antioxidants and phenolic compounds, may be slightly higher in organic wine, the differences were insignificant.[123] Researchers at the University of Geisenheim, upon conducting a review of the evidence, concluded that all the various flavor compounds and taste tests of organic versus non-organic wine are inconclusive.[124,125] The mystery of wine quality will undoubtedly go on.

For vintners, even when armed with all the information, the question of whether to certify is tricky. Some choose to farm with some of the tools in the organic toolchest, like compost or cover crops, to benefit the land while eschewing the puritanical insistence on mostly natural inputs. Others would suggest that until a winery is certified, the customer can assume that at worst, the winery is greenwashing without caring about environmental stewardship. This is why for many, the decision to go organic is about removing any doubts.

* * *

Part of what makes the question of organic wine fascinating is that it opens up a seemingly infinite Russian nesting doll of ever more complex questions. From the precise methodology of tracking chemical substances in soil to naturalistic inclinations that feel real and personal, the debate covers the full kaleidoscope of human inquiry.

In one sense, wine is an odd and inappropriate prism through which to view the larger organic story because it forgoes questions of food abundance and scarcity that feature more prominently in debates about vegetables or meat. Wine can also circumvent norms of agriculture – not so many crops regard rocky, difficult soils and low yields as desirable.

In another sense though, since wine can so readily transform into what the drinker imagines and can be seen as a reflection of human values, it provides a uniquely valuable insight into the appeal of organic farming. That organics is so often positioned as the mental stimulus to justify the imbibing of fine wine reveals that its invocation is not designed to convey practical elements of farming, but broader values of a simple agrarian life that can fill people with emotion and hope. Cynics question it. Organic growers keep shoveling compost. And for those who view the organic system as imperfect or not enough, there is another set of farming standards that brings in even more questions to ponder.

4
Biodynamics: truth or magic?

"A thoroughly healthy farm should be able to produce within itself all that it needs."[1]

"Spiritual-scientific truths are true in themselves, we need not have them confirmed by other circumstances or by external methods."[2]

Rudolf Steiner

Rudolf Steiner was an unlikely figure to foment an agrarian revolution. Born in 1861 to a telegraph operator in the Hungarian countryside, in what is now Croatia, he was drawn into theosophy, becoming an officer of the German section of the Theosophical Society in 1902. This mystical religion purported to blend occultism, Brahmanism, and Buddhism as informed by invisible Himalayan supermen and transmitted through its founder, the New Age spiritualist, psychic, and medium Helena Blavatsky. Steiner would go on to move away from theosophy, founding his own spiritual or new religion movement, anthroposophy, aimed at connecting to the spirit world.

He proselytized that "higher beings which did not belong directly to earth" had shared wisdom and power with the leaders of the Kingdom of Atlantis and they in turn had taught humans about tools, science, and art.[3] He claimed to have seen a recently deceased relative appear and speak to him, allowing him to commune with otherworldly beings, see other people's past lives, and the distant past more generally. He claimed the existence of two Jesuses, and in his book *The Occult Significance of Blood*, he professed to believing people had lost a sense of clairvoyance due to "inter-tribal mingling of bloodlines."[4]

His reputation and charismatic oratory pulled in large audiences. One first-hand account of a lecture reported that Steiner "soon holds his listeners under the spell of his power."[5] He had become a quasi-celebrity, with lines of supplicants leading to his door at all hours of the day seeking help or guidance. Steiner was nearing the end of his life by the time he turned his attention fully towards plants. His agriculture course, a series of eight lectures delivered in 1924, just five years after Fritz Haber received the Nobel Prize, was a damning critique of industrial farming and a call to re-enliven Steiner's conception of peasant farming traditions.

His talks, the written record of which exist because of notes taken by attendees, not only questioned the soundness of chemically-processed farming inputs, but went further, questioning whether spiritual reflection could do better than the scientific method. "Sulfur, carbon, hydrogen, oxygen, nitrogen: each of these materials is inwardly related to a specific spiritual principle. They are therefore very different from what our modern chemists would relate. Our chemists speak only of the corpses of the substances – not of the real substances which we must rather learn to know as sentient and living entities …"[6] By claiming that spirituality was the missing element in understanding the workings of life, he charted a course for the countermovement of a different type of agriculture.

In his agriculture course, Steiner didn't just tear down the mainstream ideas, he also proposed concoctions that could be added to manure or sprayed on plants. He told attendees they should place yarrow in a stag's bladder because the stag bladder was connected to the cosmos, which therefore enhanced the yarrow's properties. Chamomile flowers were to be encased in a cow intestine and buried over winter and oak bark was to be gathered and added to the skull of a "domestic animal." Dandelion, which Steiner called a "messenger from heaven," had to be enclosed in a cow's mesentery (the membrane connecting the bowels to the abdomen), and then buried to collect "cosmic influences."[7] All these, along with valerian, were to be added to manure, diluted, and then used for farming.

Steiner developed two more farming preparations, one manure and one quartz or silica. Each was to be stuffed into a cow horn, buried, dug back up, diluted with water, stirred in a particular way, and applied. The manure-based additive was called preparation 500 and was to be sprayed onto the soil. The silica-based additive was called preparation 501 and is sprayed onto the plant. The cow horn was deemed necessary because of its ability for "raying back whatever is life-giving and astral."[8] The agriculture course states: "If you could crawl about inside the living body of a cow – if you were there inside the belly of the cow – you would *smell* how the astral life and the living vitality pours inward from the horns. And so it is also with the hoofs."[9]

Steiner brought numerous other ideas into farming. Weaving in his anthroposophical views of astral and ego forces, Steiner described the farm as an "individuality," and said animals ought to be on the farm. To bring in outside inputs like imported manure was to "mar the working of nature." He went on to say, "… this is a perfect and self-contained cycle, which ought to be maintained, complete in itself."[10] This idea that the farm is a self-sustaining circular unit would eventually become central within the biodynamic farming point of view.

Less than a year after the lectures, Steiner would be dead. One of the mysteries that followed his death was the question of how literally to interpret his works. In the weekly news pamphlet published for members of the anthroposophical movement, Steiner wrote, "It was agreed that the information given in the lectures should be considered first of all as hints, which for the present should not be spoken of outside this circle, but looked upon as the foundation for experiments and thus gradually brought into a form suitable for publication."[11] This line has led to the interpretation of his work as fluid, scientifically testable, and non-dogmatic. His defenders can argue about his reasonableness and caution.

Another interpretation is also possible. In his closing agricultural lecture, in which Steiner had called for secrecy, he acknowledged that when information had been leaked from his past lectures, it had been viewed as "crazy."[12] In the same breath that he called for agricultural experiments to prove his theories, he expressed certainty that the experiments would undoubtedly prove his ideas,[13] which some might argue is hardly the view of an impartial scientist. His critics could argue that the notetakers who wrote down his words left us a text virtually devoid of uncertainty. Rather, consistent with Steiner's other writings, it portrays him as a clairvoyant delivering a message of "truth." In this light, Steiner's call for experiments may be best understood as a snake oil salesman's efforts to protect himself from criticism by invoking the motions of the scientific method.

The task of carrying on these secretive farming experiments fell to a cadre of Steiner followers that came to be known as the experimental circle. They invented the word biodynamics to describe Steiner's system of farming and went about testing to prove the principles and expanding on the enterprise. Copies of the agriculture course were closely guarded, with confidentiality agreements required and the first English translations going to Britain marked, "Printed for private circulation only. This copy is intended for the sole use of the person above-named."[14] In its early form, the movement searched for focus. The idea of the farm as an organism was not yet central. In 1928 an organization called Demeter was formed to create standards for this new conception of farming.

Steiner had a headquarters of sorts built in Dornach, Switzerland, which he called the Goetheanum, named after Johann Wolfgang von Goethe. It was intended to be a place where anthroposophical thinkers could discuss and promote their ideas, and one of the people who was welcomed there was Ehrenfried Pfeiffer. Arriving in 1921 at the age of 20, Pfeiffer started out working in the lighting department, but he went on to agricultural research, eventually writing a book on biodynamic experiments and progress. Even as he wrote in 1938, secrecy was still important to the movement. Directions on how to make a collection of biodynamic preparations could only be given to "bona fide biodynamic farmers of standing."[15] But his explanation of biodynamics was a significant change from Steiner. Gone were the regular references of anthroposophical ego and ether bodies and astral forces. Instead, Pfeiffer's book was more scientific, reviewing experiments on biodynamics such as bathing seeds in biodynamic preparations and observing the plant[16] or dividing a pot into two compartments, one with "untreated compost" and the other with biodynamically prepared compost, and observing root growth.[17] Pfeiffer's biodynamic vision included values too. He called for a back-to-the-land movement celebrating independent farmers, soil fertility, and a love of work.[18]

Apart from Pfeiffer, another of the important Steiner acolytes was Maria Thun. A German gardener who became obsessed with biodynamics in the mid-twentieth century, Thun was a prolific force. She experimented and observed plants for years, creating myriad farming principles that took root in the biodynamic movement. One such principle stated that plants should not be sown and planted on Good Friday and Easter Sunday, noting "The events at Golgotha [Jesus's crucifixion] which took place 2,000 years ago still affect the earth each year. The plant-world is sensitive to this."[19] One teaching that attracted more followers was the idea that by looking at which astrological constellation the moon was in, she could divide all days into root, leaf, flower, and fruit days. This could in turn determine which crops to pick at which times and later was used to determine when wines are drinking best. Some biodynamic practitioners employ Thun's prescriptions and claim they work, but the Demeter international certification standards have no reference to root, leaf, flower, and fruit days.

Biodynamics has evolved considerably in the century since Steiner lectured. Aurélie Truffat, of Demeter France, says that the international standards for biodynamics change as often as every year.[20] One significant recent addition was the requirement that a farm must have 10 percent of its land undisturbed by farming. Biodynamics has become inflected with the ideas of ecologically-minded farmers, such as cover crops, natural ingredients, and low-emission farming. Demeter now uses organics as a minimum standard. Seen in this light, biodynamics is less of a monolithic entity and more a collection of farming theories housed under one roof that can all be evaluated independently, some of them coming and going, some of them new, some of them old. The philosophy behind it has adjusted over time as well; Steiner's idea of the farm as a living organism and individuality was not at the forefront of the experimental phase that immediately followed his death, but it re-emerged later as a central tenet of the biodynamic philosophy and brand. Another older idea still present is homeopathy, which involves diluting something with water until there is hardly a trace of the compound left. It doesn't relate as much to wine, but to illustrate the point, Demeter's guidelines state, "homeopathic remedies in place of vaccines are strongly recommended."[21]

Slowly, vintners took notice. A few at first, building into a movement of wineries around the world. Demeter claims a growing number of biodynamic wineries, 1,439 as of 2024, with 26,556 hectares (65,621 acres) under biodynamic management or in conversion to Demeter standard.[22] Biodyvin, a European based biodynamic group, claims 225 wine growers as of 2025.[23] Biodynamic vineyards make up a minuscule percentage of total acreage, but the conversation about them in the wine world takes up much more intellectual space, particularly in the high-end wine scene. In wine bars and Michelin-starred restaurants, sommeliers can be heard murmuring to their patrons that this producer or that practices biodynamics.

Today, several organizations create and implement biodynamic standards. To study the standards, we can look at Demeter and Biodyvin, two certifying agencies that differ on what is permitted. Unlike Demeter, which certifies all types of agriculture, Biodyvin focuses on certifying vineyards, and has decided that due to the difficulty of adding herd animals to certain vineyards, standards on the need for keeping farm animals on site can be looser. Given Steiner's vision that each farm should be a self-sufficient organism, the challenge to certifiers is how strictly to hold to that vision. Even the Demeter rules allow for purchased inputs in certain instances. Regardless of what the certifying authorities say, biodynamic vignerons differ on how strictly to interpret the principle that all inputs should derive from the farm itself.

In broad simplification, a biodynamic vineyard is one in which the farmer follows organic standards, has the goal of circular farming, generally incorporates animals, and uses the biodynamic preparations. Since biodynamic certification requires organic certification as a starting point, researchers have come around to the principle that to prove any efficacy of biodynamic farming, it should be compared to organics to ensure the causal variable is biodynamic and not organic. Some researchers have stated that the best way to differentiate between the two is the inclusion of the biodynamic preparations, while others argue the biodynamic philosophy is much more significant and any attempt to compare organics and biodynamics must go beyond the biodynamic amendments. Since academic research has lagged on biodynamics for years, the first testing grounds for the practice have been the vineyards of biodynamics converts.

* * *

"When truth is in a product, it sells itself,"[24] Nicolas Joly proclaims. Joly has been one of the most vocal advocates for biodynamic viticulture and, together with his daughter Virginie, he oversees Coulée de Serrant in France's Loire Valley. The vineyard is enclosed by ancient walls and was first planted by

Cistercian monks in the twelfth century. Having been an early adopter of biodynamics, Coulée de Serrant is one of the more historically significant vineyards that has been converted. Joly explains his understanding of how one of the biodynamic preparations works:

> *That's why after the big storm – when was it – in '89 or something – people were finding deers which were dead of emotion. So, you see that the deer is intensely linked to perception and emotion. What is the end of the process of emotion? ... You have it in the kidney process. And at the end, the kidney is finally cleaning the body, and it ends in a bladder. So when we take the bladder of a deer, and put inside yarrow, which has huge properties to act on the kidneys ... you are just catching the forces of the deer and you put yarrow hanged outside, et cetera, et cetera, – in a bladder. If it is well done, when you have the treatment which is spread on vineyards it's a huge reception to Venus forces because Venus is a planet, you know ... of emotions ... So you are just carrying more toward your place, the forces of Venus. Behind each preparation you have a link to one planet.*[25]

Joly, a self-described anthroposophist, embraces the argument as made by Steiner in the 1924 lectures, and as such could be described as an originalist. Over the century since Steiner's passing, others have entered the biodynamic movements and the understanding and justifications for how biodynamics supposedly works has shifted.

Across the world, in California, another certified biodynamic winery reveals a different understanding. Rodrigo Soto is a talented winemaker working at Quintessa Winery in Napa. Soto became seriously interested in pursuing biodynamics after attending a tasting of biodynamically versus organically grown wines. "We got all the Avengers there," he remarked jokingly, noting the number and caliber of the celebrity vignerons in attendance. He reports that all of them preferred the biodynamic wine. Soto does not talk about theosophy and planets, his focus is on soil fertility and good wine. "Part of the problem of the miscommunication about biodynamics is that people immediately talk about the moon cycles or one or two of the preps and I think that deteriorates the image of biodynamic farming because it makes people believe that this is all voodoo,"[26] he says.

In terms of the practical effects of the biodynamic preparations, Soto views them as inoculating the fermenting compost, which, when spread, will help soil nutrients become more available to the vines. Soil science clearly shows that not all nutrients present in soil are available to be taken up by plants. In Soto's telling, this is biodynamic farming's solution to the issue.

Soto also believes that biodynamics has helped to create a closer relationship between the farmer and the land. For the biodynamic preparation 500, which is manure placed in a horn and buried in winter, and the 501 preparation, which is silica placed in a horn and buried in the summer, dilution is required; both are mixed with copious quantities of water and stirred in a specific way for an hour to "dynamize" the solution, Soto explains:

> *The concept is that you dynamize them yourself in order to do a couple of things ... That oxygenation is going to potentiate it, and make it stronger, just like the homeopathy principles, but also, in theory, you're getting into a state of meditation, that, through the force of your arm, you're conducting the energy that is necessary to potentiate the substance ... and then that substance is going to get applied to all your property ... And I like that idea a lot because at the very end ... it creates an intimate relationship with the property that you're working with because you are in theory present in all of it.*[27]

The idea of treating biodynamics as a way to be present and more observant of the farm is a firmly practical argument, allowing those who are not persuaded by the spiritual argument to understand how there might be effects on the vines. If the preparations act as a ritualistic practice that encourages vintners to walk their vineyards, then perhaps this is part of the causal explanation for the results seen.

Craig Camp, a winery General Manager in Applegate Valley, in the Pacific northwest, works biodynamically because he thinks there is demonstrable scientific thinking behind the inclusion of animals on the vineyard and allowance for biodiversity. He thinks a schism has opened up between different schools of biodynamic vintners, observing, "I don't know if there'll ever be a reconciliation between the anthroposophy side and the practical side because it's really a different thing."[28]

Still, as Soto implies, even the biodynamic vineyards that speak in the vocabulary of measurable effects and scientific rigor use the biodynamic preparations, relying on vineyard additives that developed within the homeopathic method and for this there has emerged a field of scientific literature to see if it is possible to account for any effect the preparations have. The primary claims that emerge from the various practitioners of the biodynamic community are that it is better for the environment, better for the soil, and better for the wine.

Dr. John Reganold, who holds a soil science PhD from UC Davis, has spent most of his career researching and teaching in the College of Agricultural, Human, and Natural Resource Sciences at Washington State University. Reganold admires the biodynamic pioneer Ehrenfried Pfeiffer, but was skeptical of the scientific credibility of his and some other original biodynamic research. Risking career and reputation, he set out to bring biodynamic studies to mainstream journals, publishing a paper in *Science* in 1993 comparing biodynamic farms to conventional ones.[29] He recalls, "So I was comparing biodynamic with conventional, and what I found was the soil – every case – it kicked ass ... but that was biodynamic against conventional and I never could say the preps worked."[30]

Curious to determine if credible science could demonstrate a difference between a biodynamic and an organic site, he embarked on another study in California, focusing on the biodynamic amendments. After thoroughly profiling the soil, vines, and fruit at each site, he found there were some differences "small and of doubtful practical significance," or no differences at all.[31] Turning the grapes into wine, they had a taste-off set up to see if there was a difference: "… we didn't find really any difference that way," he says matter-of-factly.[32] A separate meta-review that came out in 2019 similarly found no taste difference within the research literature, stating "No overall differences in berry composition or juice and wine quality among management systems could be observed."[33]

Though Reganold didn't find a difference in his study, many practitioners argue that taste is affected. Some explicitly state that biodynamic practices make the wine better while others suggest that although they are not sure why, biodynamic wines seem to taste better. A *Washington Post* headline summarizes this argument, "Biodynamic wine has roots in pseudoscience, but the proof is in the bottle."[34] Some argue that the fact that many of the world's most respected producers are biodynamic is some degree of vindication for the idea. The critics of biodynamics might argue that these wineries have the extra disposable income to collect environmental credentials to market their wine, but the quality came before the farming conversation, not after. It's biodynamic's chicken or egg question – what came first, the cow horn or the aromatic bouquet? There have been some tasting panel studies showing some respondents highlighting differences between organic and biodynamic wines, but the differences were generally minimal, without showing biodynamic superiority.[35]

Another factor cited as a reason to transition to biodynamics is the encouragement of root growth. In his book on biodynamic farming, *A Biodynamic Manual, Practical Instructions for Farmers and Gardeners*, the biodynamic consultant Pierre Masson suggested that the biodynamic cow manure preparation encourages root growth, encourages microbial activity, and alters soil pH, among other properties. The root growth claim has been supported by respected vintners, such as Dominique Lafon.[36] There is a critique of this viewpoint, that this is merely repeating the claims made by some of the original biodynamic advocates but without the proof to back it up. Dr. Megan Bartlett, a plant biologist at UC Davis, contests the efficacy of preparations relying on active ingredients diluted to the degree that the biodynamic preparations are, stating, "There's not really a physical principle where the biodynamic preparations would cause deeper root growth because most of them are at homeopathic concentrations, so they're essentially water."[37] This larger critique of biodynamics, that the preparations don't have a causal theory, might indicate that in cases where a grower does observe a difference, it might be because of variables unrelated to biodynamics. Due to the difficulty of measuring complex phenomena, Bartlett concludes that individual studies showing biodynamic effects are "within the realm of experimental noise."[38]

* * *

One of the people who has come to embrace biodynamics because of his own findings is Olivier Humbrecht of Domaine Zind-Humbrecht in Alsace, France. Humbrecht holds degrees in agriculture and enology and is the president of Biodyvin, the biodynamic wine grower organization. His family has been in the wine business for four centuries. His discovery of biodynamics happened through compost. While paying a contractor to redistribute various composts to his vineyards, Humbrecht saw that the man had stopped, and was going through the compost with bags, collecting something. "What are you doing?" asked Hubrecht. The contractor explained that he was a fisherman, and was collecting worms – he had noticed there were many more worms in one compost compared to the other – in fact, it was the most worms the contractor had seen in any compost. Inquiring about the origin of the compost, Humbrecht discovered that it had been prepared biodynamically and sold without marketing it as such. Humbrecht had the biodynamic and organic composts compared in a laboratory and was told that the biodynamic one had a million times the microorganisms compared to the other one. "I said, damn, it is a massive difference."[39] It's these sorts of observations that led Humbrecht to slowly come around to biodynamics.

One of the studies Humbrecht cites on the fungal distinctiveness of biodynamic soil was co-authored by Ignacio Belda, currently a professor of microbiology at the Complutense University of Madrid. Belda and his colleagues collected 350 soil samples, half from Spanish and half from American vineyards, and analyzed the fungal structure. They found that biodynamic sites had a different arrangement of fungal associations relative to conventional sites, and even somewhat more than organic.[40] Belda, though excited about the potential of the paper, is cautious about overhyping the results for biodynamics compared to organics. "In my paper, we don't say that it's better. We just say that it changed the structure of fungal communities. We don't even know if this different structure is better or worse than the other."[41]

Asked if he could tell what was causing the differences in fungal structure between conventional, organic, and biodynamic vineyards, Belda replied he didn't know what the causal variable was, but he did have some skepticism about the biodynamic amendments. "I also believe that it is not those microorganisms coming from the cow shit that change the microbiome of the entire vineyard soil ... the microbiome of soils are pretty resilient to changes." Belda is alluding to the idea that the microbiome of the soil is hard to change and that it is not as sensitive as some think.

As biodynamic practitioners are quick to admit, their holistic farming philosophy contains many elements, and they can now argue that the soil microbiome may be distinct in some way, but explaining how that works is difficult. Critics of biodynamics can focus on the lack of empirical evidence that this change has a tangible impact on farming and the lack of causal understanding. Defenders can posit that this study helps show that biodynamics as it's run in reality does have a different effect on the soil compared to other farming systems.

Another scientific attempt to better understand the vineyard and soil difference of a biodynamic vineyard compared to organic and conventional quietly began on 1 hectare of land (2.47 acres) near the Rhine river in Germany in 2006. Dr. Randolph Kauer, a longtime professor of viticulture at Germany's pre-eminent winemaking school, Geisenheim University, was interested in studying biodynamics, though he acknowledges the risk of this decision. "When you visit your colleagues in other universities and you start to talk about biodynamic agriculture and Rudolf Steiner … it's not always easy. Then you're not a serious scientist," Kauer says.[42]

Whereas Belda's research focused on the real-world vineyards, Kauer planted his own research vineyard in Rheingau, dividing the block into conventional, organic, and biodynamic. By establishing all sub-blocks simultaneously on one plot and planting everything in the same way and to the same variety (Riesling), Kauer was better prepared to account for real-world challenges like variable disease status, soil type, vine age, vine architecture, and so on.

Kauer and his colleagues tested the site against a broad array of soil parameters: soil organic carbon as a measure of health and fertility, soil bulk density to measure compaction, available water capacity to see how the soil would do in times of drought, and more. After reviewing the results to date, he shares that there "has never been a thing that shows organic is better than biodynamic or biodynamic is better than organic," and references soil microbial analysis showing no significant differences between the fungal and bacterial populations in the soil of the organically and biodynamically managed subplots.[43]

Jean-Michel Florin still sees the value in biodynamics. Raised on a biodynamic farm in the north of France, Florin became a chief organizer of the French biodynamic movement, ultimately rising to become a co-leader of the division of agriculture at the Goetheanum, Rudolf Steiner's school of spiritual science. He is a prolific writer, and is known for his book *Biodynamic Wine Growing: Understanding the vine and its rhythms*. Addressing the state of research on biodynamics, he notes his approach, "On one side I look at the results of research on the other side … I try to make my own picture." Florin believes that biodynamic farming increases the quality of produce, noting, "One day was OK … and the other day was a moon node. And none of us knew, only the guy who brought the carrots. And we made a short comparison – the color, the shine, the shape, the taste, the smell, and so on – twenty people together, and we made the summary and the difference was so obvious."[44]

Florin says that he has seen a lot of situations like this, and some in the biodynamic community share his perspective that these lived examples, rather than scientific studies, help prove the biodynamic case. Stories of vineyards coming back to life after biodynamic farming began and something in the soil changing once the preps were added are still a drumbeat in the community.

The reference to the moon alludes to an original Steiner belief that the moon affects how plants grow and that farming should take the moon into account when making decisions. Biodynamic growers have differing opinions on the importance of the moon. The 191-page document of international biodynamic standards has no references to the moon, despite Steiner's exhortations. Asked about the absence of moon forces in the current international biodynamic guidelines, Aurélie Truffat of Demeter France said, "There was no study showing that the moon cycles are effective … There was only the work of Maria Thun, but in short, it's not considered scientific research."[45] Further augmenting this point was a literature review conducted in 2020 by Spanish researchers which lambasts the idea of lunar farming:

> We found that there is no reliable, science-based evidence for any relationship between lunar phases and plant physiology in any plant-science related textbooks or peer-reviewed journal articles justifying agricultural practices conditioned by the moon. Nor does evidence from the field of physics support a causal relationship between lunar forces and plant responses.[46]

Some biodynamic vignerons continue to farm this way and they call it biodynamic farming. This further splitting of beliefs within the biodynamic movement underlies the difficulty in finding a singular type of biodynamic farming to compare to organics for research.

One of the people not buying any of it is Linda Chalker-Scott. A horticulture PhD and Extension Education specialist, she is the editor of the *Journal of the National Association of County Agricultural Agents*, the western chapter of the International Society of Arboriculture, a professional trade magazine, and is the author of a scientific literature review on biodynamic farming. "I got into what I do because I figured it was one of the less controversial things to work on ... And what I've discovered is that, as with politics, when people have emotional ties to a belief, it's very hard to get them to step away from that belief."[47]

When asked why people are drawn to biodynamics, Linda rattles off a well-rehearsed list of traits she finds often draw people into what she describes as pseudoscience: the cachet of foreignness, the appeal of ancient knowledge, the rejection of mainstream practices, the fear of anything chemical, and the back-to-the-land appeal. "When it's pointed out that there isn't any support behind it, people tend to dig their heels in," she says. She also shares that she and a number of colleagues believe that organics, regardless of its merits, is no longer the shiny, new agricultural practice and therefore biodynamics has been able to step into that role, becoming the new, mystical alternative. "It's a great marketing tool," she says matter-of-factly. Asked about the papers that have shown that there are some differences between biodynamics and organics, Chalker-Scott responds: "... given that the bulk of work on BD [biodynamics] does not support the hypothesis (i.e., that biodynamic preparations have a significant effect on plants or soils), contrary research must meet a high bar to merit consideration."[48]

* * *

The question of soil quality is central to biodynamics, but other environmental questions are also worth asking. Does biodynamics allow for more ecological diversity or emit less greenhouse gas compared to organics? In a 2019 review meta-paper, entitled "Organic and biodynamic viticulture affect biodiversity and properties of vine and wine: A systematic quantitative review," the authors reported that biodynamics carried "substantially lower environmental burdens,"[49] citing a Spanish study published in 2014. The paper reported the "lowest environmental burdens" even including an organic site for comparison.[50]

One of the researchers involved in that study is Spanish-born Ian Vásquez-Rowe, who lives in Peru. He and his co-authors used life cycle assessment of biodynamic and conventional viticulture in northwest Spain to try to understand the environmental impact. "Life cycle assessment can be quite sloppy sometimes, with uncertainties,"[51] Vásquez-Rowe acknowledges, and explains that models have come a long way in the last decade.

Due to the expense and logistical difficulty of measuring the emissions and effects of farm inputs for every study, scientists can choose from various emissions models and databases. Some models are created by independent academics, some by the Intergovernmental Panel on Climate Change within the United Nations. Choosing between these models was the first challenge for Vásquez-Rowe and his colleagues.

For example, the model he used wasn't able to account for copper and sulfur, two of the farm inputs that most biodynamic growers rely on to combat undesirable fungal growths on vine. The study also points out that because of the complex way in which copper interacts with the soil and because "the retention rate of the soil for these pesticides is very high" the researchers assumed that they wouldn't contribute to air and water emissions.[52] Similarly, they chose only to account for the transportation and spreading, but not the fertilizer creation, since it was assumed to be the fecal by-product of existing operations.[53] This raises the question of how to account for vineyards that bring in sheep expressly for the purpose of making wine.

Another intellectual challenge is what Vásquez-Rowe calls multifunctionality. If a sheep is on a vineyard, a practice strongly encouraged in biodynamics, it provides manure and weeding services for the vineyard, but also produces milk or wool that can be sold separately. When accounting for the transporting and spreading of manure, researchers need to decide how to allocate the greenhouse gas emissions so as to avoid double counting. Additionally, the biodynamic winery in the study stated their soils didn't need compost, so the researchers didn't measure for spreading this,[54] but most other biodynamic farms do spread compost, so the question arises how representative the vineyard in this study was. These and many other difficulties make it hard to perfectly measure the greenhouse gas effects of different farming systems.[55]

Biodynamic producers can claim that decreased farm inputs and the more holistic view of the farm lower their emissions and raise ecological diversity. Critics of biodynamics claim that including livestock in crop production adds more net methane while simultaneously producing lower crop yields due to inputs of questionable effect at a time when inefficient agriculture is already causing global harm. The juxtaposition of these viewpoints isn't meant to imply false equivalency, but merely present the arguments of both sides and to illustrate why researchers find it difficult to accurately measure holistic impacts.

* * *

There are two prisms through which to praise or condemn biodynamics. It can be judged based on the total effect it has had on farming over the course of its century-long existence, including all the beliefs from the past. Or it can be judged solely based on the current standards as stated by Demeter or other certifying agencies.

For those in support of the idea of biodynamics, the result is better soil, better ecology, and better wine, but there is also the positive social outcome of what biodynamics has done for the world. With the emergence and success of Demeter, Steiner and biodynamics birthed an idea within the twentieth century that food and wine could be held to higher standards than what the government sets. This has launched a host of other standards competing for attention from the wine consumer that have raised awareness and demand for climate-friendly practices. That the organic standard owes existential thanks to biodynamics is certainly a point in its favor for many people.

Countermovements in wine eco-certification like Regenerative Organic Certified (ROC) have emerged, challenging the notion that biodynamic preparations have a place in the modern wine world. Some might argue that what ROC appears to be doing is stripping biodynamics of its mysticism and focusing on ecological outcomes. Some might view these movements as superior to biodynamics because they are more scientific, and others still defend biodynamics, suggesting that the proof is in the wine or the values.

For those on the side of biodynamics, those values are important. The principle that a farm, or a vineyard, should be its own cohesive ecosystem without outside inputs is a hard-to-attain goal, but one worth striving for. On the one hand, there may be the ecological arguments, that when done well it has a lighter impact on the land than most of the rest of viticulture, but there are also the ideals embedded within it. For many, the principle of a small, independent, naturally-inclined vineyard is worth fighting for. To these people, the resulting wine is more honest and authentic.

And for those who remain unconvinced of the values or efficacy of the farming, there is the final defense, that it does not do any harm. The amendments don't pollute the environment, the wine isn't toxic – there is no problem. Others contend that espousing unscientific ideas does do harm. Linda Chalker-Scott summarizes this view: "… when these things are promoted … as being better than conventional … without any kind of scientific evidence, then it does exacerbate those differences where people become less and less trustful of science."[56] She goes on to list vaccines, GMOs (genetically modified organisms), and climate change as issues on which public viewpoints don't always line up with the scientific consensus and where this lack of trust in science has resulted in tangible harm.

Still, many are unsure what the right path is. Part of the reason there is so much uncertainty is that biodynamics and organics are continually changing, as both farming principles adapt to new times, and farming fads come and go. Some of the researchers who have studied biodynamics say that there is much more research needed, and more research can still help.

In his introduction to one of his books, *An Outline of Occult Science*, Steiner notes why his audience was drawn to the topic: "… what attracts many adherents of occult science – or occultism – is nothing but the fatal craving for what is unknown and mysterious or even vague."[57] One could ask whether the same attraction is true of biodynamic farming, whether adherents are moved by core ideas that feel important and true, and are justified with the level of scientific rigor available at the time. Or maybe the popularity of biodynamic principles like natural remedies, holistic perspectives, self sufficiency, and circular, animal-inclusive viticulture, is also a reaction to the modern world. Whatever vintners decide to do, they will need to make sure that their farming system can stand the test of time.

5
Climate and wine – holding on

"Men argue. Nature acts."

Voltaire, Philosophical Dictionary[1]

It is difficult to find a winemaker who has more experience making wine at the highest level than Jean-Claude Berrouet. Born in occupied France during World War II, he learned under the celebrated wine professor Émile Peynaud, and became Technical Director of Établissements Jean-Pierre Moueix in the early sixties. Entrusted with the winemaking job at Château Petrus, one of the more revered wineries in the world, Berrouet is one of the most experienced palates when it comes to assessing how wine has changed over three quarters of a century.

Opening the large wooden gates of his winery cellar in the small village of Montagne-Saint-Émilion, his view is an eleventh-century church tower breaching a sea of vines. With its long history, the town is an ideal place to think deeply about how wine has changed in the last century and what might happen in the next. It was 1990 when Berrouet first noticed changes. Not only were alcohol levels creeping higher, acidity dropping lower, and tannins getting softer, but vintners would go on to discover wider and more mysterious effects of climate on the flavor of wine.

Of course, the climate had been changing for some time. France only began its modern conception of wine regions in 1935 with the creation of the National Institute for Origin and Quality (INAO). It would be just three years later, in 1938, that Guy Stewart Callendar became the first to demonstrate conclusively that the surface of the earth was warming.[2] In the same decade that France adopted its most serious legal framework for protecting regional wine taste typicity as special and worth fighting for, the world learned that those regional taste identities might be subject to change at a global scale.

Seeing the effects of climate change on his grapes, Berrouet chose not to let his winemaking practices stagnate. He used less new oak and more clay vessels, shifting his focus to enhancing freshness. Historically, Bordeaux winemakers added sugar in cold vintages, which adds alcohol and body, therefore increasing deliciousness. Now, the practice is much rarer.

The dilemmas that Berrouet faces in Montagne-Saint-Émilion are a microcosm of what the rest of the wine world is experiencing. There are many questions raised by the specter of climate change but a key one for global wine drinkers is whether climate change will challenge the supremacy of certain established growing regions over others.

* * *

Not far away from Berrouet, at Bordeaux Sciences Agro, a professor of viticulture has been hard at work trying to understand what climate change means not only for that region's producers, but for the whole world. Kees van Leeuwen has worked on over one hundred peer reviewed papers and is considered one of the foremost experts on terroir and the effect of climate on vineyards. His 2024 literature review, which he co-authored along with several other academics, sent a tremor through the wine world when it reported that by the end of the twenty-first century, traditional European wine-growing regions might shrink by 20 to 70 percent.[3] Reflecting on the possibility of vintners trying to adapt their vineyards to recreate the types of wines that came before, van Leeuwen pronounces, "You can change some practices in trying to push it back a little bit, but you will never go back all the way."[4]

Understanding the historical context of how certain sites came to represent quality in Bordeaux helps with comprehending the implications of climate change around the world. In the right bank of Bordeaux, which is known for Merlot-based blends, the crown jewels – according to market value for wine – are Saint-Émilion and Pomerol. Van Leeuwen and one of his PhD students showed that the lesser-known satellites around Saint-Émilion were cooler,[5, 6] which may explain why they did not develop to be as prestigious as the towns their names suggest they orbit. "Now they are definitely catching up," he says, though other factors like soil, elevation, and vineyard management make prediction difficult. He also suspects that western Bordeaux, which is closer to the ocean, will have the potential to increase in quality.[7]

More broadly throughout history, southern and western facing slopes performed better because they received more sun, but now, given the increasing spectre of heatwaves associated with climate change, the exact blessing that their ancestors were grateful for might fill a modern Bordelais vigneron with angst. The sun also burns.

Though achieving enough ripeness to ensure quality has been the goal for centuries, there were early clues that some of the better suited sites were better protected in years when heatwaves did strike. In speaking of work he did with his PhD student, Laure de Rességuier, van Leeuwen notes, "We saw that on the limestone plateaus in Saint-Émilion, where they produce the best wines – so Ausone, Canon, Clos Fourtet, Pavie – in fact, the maximum temperatures are lower because it's just more windy."[8] This finding raises the question of whether factors like wind might shield some regions against the particularly damaging effects of a heating planet or whether even these revered sites will be undeniably altered – and perhaps for the worse.

Others argue that climate change will be even more severe, going much further than affecting wine flavor. This position was laid out in 2013 when Lee Hannah, who holds a doctorate in environmental science and engineering, published a paper with several colleagues that grappled with the implications of climate change in wine. In a scenario where climate change accelerated rapidly – a not unlikely possibility – the researchers estimated that classic wine regions would lose 25–73 percent of their land, claiming that it would become unsuitable for grapes. Hannah noted that grapes grown in warmer climates need more water and so vineyard owners trying to maintain their crop in the face of climate change might further burden water resources.[9]

Using the example of Chile, a country with a rich and thriving wine growing history, Hannah and his colleagues stated that 95 percent of the wine growing regions of Chile are already under water stress and that climate change could further exacerbate the problem. With predictions of decreased rainfall and dwindling snowpack in the Andes Mountains, a bleak picture emerges of an already threatened region pushed to the brink.

In addition to making these pessimistic projections for much of the current wine world, Hannah and his colleagues went on to suggest a series of new regions that would be suitable for wine. In short, he predicts a march towards the poles. In the northern hemisphere, England and the Canada–U.S. border area around the Rocky Mountains would be amongst the winners and in the southern hemisphere, Tasmania and Patagonia could become larger players in the quality wine world.

The implication for long-standing wine regions is clear – not only should the wine consumer question the extent to which the wines taste as they historically have and if they can maintain their cultural character, but she must also question whether wine regions in these places can continue to be as sustainable as they have been in the past. The implicit challenge to vintners is to what extent they can adapt to ensure their vines remain protected.

The paper not only critiques the potentially greater environmental footprint of existing wine regions under climate change but also elucidates how new vineyard plantings towards the poles could be harmful. Any agriculture, including grapevines, impinging on native habitat is seen as an ecological loss for flora and fauna. In China, which the paper predicts will become a better wine region, Hannah and his co-authors point out that these agriculturally undeveloped regions are currently habitat for the Giant Panda and vineyard expansion might therefore be harmful.[10]

This paper caused a notable stir, and Kees van Leeuwen was one of several academics to write a response, stating that its predictions of the demise of current wine regions went too far. Pointing out methodological errors, they castigated the paper, claiming that several regions in France are growing wine successfully and sustainably despite being within Hannah's "unsuitable" range. They left some of the environmental impact claims unchallenged.[11]

Other burgeoning wine regions might view further vineyard expansion as a boon rather than a harm. In the United Kingdom, where tentative plantings of early-ripening varieties have been increasing, many vineyards are planted on existing farmland, replacing one crop with another, so claiming that local species are being negatively impacted would be a stretch. The same is possible for other regions with existing agriculture. Additionally, regulation and responsible vintners may limit the expansion of new vineyards into virgin forest, decreasing the impact and likelihood of new plantings.

Some may further criticize the Hannah study, citing these circumstances as a reason to doubt the possibility of species loss. And any new vineyard plantings might have the positive effect of enlivening local cultures and reinforcing economic stability. But others would argue that there are already examples where vineyards have been expanded into unsuitable locations, causing environmental damage, and we will continue to see how it plays out as temperatures rise around the world.

At Bordeaux Sciences Agro, a different set of tools is being used to assess the suitability of vineyard land in a warming world where more water might be required. Gregory Gambetta is a Californian who settled in France to continue a prolific career in wine research. With a doctorate in plant biology from UC Davis, his focus is entirely on evaluating grapevines through observation.

One of Gambetta's worries is that certain regions could lose the ability to grow vines sustainably in the face of climate change. "I mean, if you're depleting groundwater to the point where the earth is sinking, and you're losing aquifer volume and stuff like this, you're not doing it right."[12] An expert in the adaptability of vines to water stress, Gambetta can see both sides of the coin – the downsides of continuing to farm grapes in places where there is insufficient water available as well as the upsides of bringing more irrigation to Europe, where dry farming has been the norm and is closely regulated.

"If there's a really extreme heatwave or something like that, you definitely are going to preserve the health of the vineyard – you want to give those vines water,"[13] Gambetta notes. But he is keenly aware of the practical effects of legalizing irrigation in existing wine regions. Growers know that irrigating vines can increase their yields, a temptation hard to ignore once Pandora's box has been opened. "You know, then growers will use it," Gambetta acknowledges.[14]

In Spain, vineyards used to be almost universally dry farmed, but now 50 percent are irrigated.[15] On the one hand, this can be viewed as a blow to Spain's viticulture, indicating that the region is no longer as well adapted to vines. On the other hand, it can be seen as a helpful adaptation for farmers, allowing them to keep their vines healthy, and considering that vines use less water than many other crops, they can argue it's better to preserve vines than to switch to another crop that takes more water and more pesticides. Others might argue that vines are a luxury crop, and that switching to staple crops would be the way forward, though this of course raises the question of what is luxury and what is necessity.

Even this is difficult to measure, though. Some regions, with plenty of available water, may increase carbon dioxide emissions from the transportation of water to their vineyards, where no water was needed before. In the grand scheme of emissions this may be small, but it has an effect, and the wine community will have to decide at what point the collective emissions and energy of wine regions would be deemed too much.

Critics contend that sites for grapevines should be limited to dry farming only, so as to not put any pressure on aquifers. As pressure builds, these places should move away from viticulture. Defenders argue that mitigatory efforts are being put in place to preserve water in the soil and reduce water use to the point that it's not a burden on aquifers – soil moisture probes, drip irrigation, cover crops, drought-tolerant rootstocks, and many other adaptations are being implemented. The question is whether these mitigations are enough to offset the increased water demands plants will exert.

* * *

Across the world, another wine region is coming to grips with the implications of climate change. The discovery of gold in California in 1848 may have garnered more attention in the press, but winegrowing in the Golden State, which predates the Declaration of Independence, would ultimately take on greater cultural importance. In 1862, when the United States was engulfed in civil war, the French journal *Revue Viticole* saw fit to comment on the state of American viticulture, noting "Californie's" ideal climate for vines and declaring that they were the only wines in America that could compete with European wine.[16]

After a visit in 1881, a horticulture professor from Missouri upended his academic life and moved west to become a vintner, explaining that California was "destined to be the vine land of the world … We have the finest climate in the world and can always make a good product even in the most unfavorable seasons."[17] The dawn of Californian viticulture promised a different kind of gold, the whole premise of which rested on a finely tuned and delicate climatic balance.

In the twenty-first century, Californians have begun to grapple with what climate change means for their backyard. At first there was a sense that climate change might be a boon for many of the state's varied grape-growing climates. Between 1951 and 1997, there was increased sugar maturity and higher quality wines, and given the observed 14 percent increase in growing degree days over this period, climate change was suspected to be the causal force.[18] Before 1976 frosts were reported more regularly, with poor wine quality ratings as a result, but after 1976 frosts became much less common.[19]

Julian Alston, the distinguished professor emeritus in the Agricultural and Resource Economics Department at UC Davis and director of the Robert Mondavi Institute Center for Wine Economics, and Sarah Smith, a postdoctoral scholar specializing in the microeconomics of agriculture and resources, are less optimistic.

Alston and Smith distributed a working paper in agricultural economics in which they tried to account for the randomness of climate change. Rather than measuring the mean average temperature, which has been the usual tool of agricultural climatologists, the researchers looked at how the market was affected by what happens in the extreme events that are expected to come more often.

Although many farmers might not need an economist to tell them a heatwave is bad for vines, it is difficult to understand what extreme weather may do to wine prices. By getting granular about pricing and temperatures, Alston and Smith attempted to measure how hot a heatwave needed to get to change wine prices. Using a large database of Californian wines sold on the secondary market, Alston and Smith found that as degree days above 35°C (95°F) increased, wine prices decreased and critical appraisals of the vintage went down.[20]

The difficulty that any economist will readily admit is that wine pricing and vintage scores may be a poor proxy for wine quality, but in a world where wine quality is so hard to measure, particularly over time as tastes and styles change, its value may be better than nothing.

One of the challenges of correlating global warming to qualitative changes in wine is accounting for all the variables. For example, during the second half of the twentieth century, when some research found promise in climate change, there had been a concurrent investment of brains and money reforming California's "wild west" viticulture, which could also account for some of the improvements seen across wines over that period. Similarly, as critics such as the notable Robert Parker awarded high scores to riper wine styles, many sought to emulate these wines, making it difficult to tease apart the impacts of a warming climate from a cultural pursuit of ripeness.

Looking at long-term climate models and assuming no adaptive changes from growers, Alston and Smith predict that Napa Valley Cabernet prices will decrease. Alston poses the question: "The projected climate for end-of-century in the Napa Valley is Fresno and so the question to ask a winemaker is to say, well, do you think you could make wine anything like the quality you're making in Napa today in Fresno?"[21]

The use of Fresno as an example is not accidental. A part of the San Joaquin Valley of central California, this hot inner plain produces 100 percent of the state's raisins, a hint at its status as a place known for inexpensive wine. The implication that Napa's climate would mirror Fresno's is devastating. Sarah Smith is cautious, and qualifies their findings, "You have to assume there's no adaptation, and that's a very strong assumption. We do think that there will be a lot of adaptation."[22]

The question for wineries is when or whether to make the supreme form of adaptation – a switch to another grape variety. Gregory Jones, a world-renowned climatologist specializing in grapevines, has plotted the main wine varieties on a spectrum of average growing season temperatures based on where they are currently grown, with Müller-Thurgau at the coolest end and Nebbiolo at the hottest.[23] In a purely analytical world, grape growers could use the tool to see where their climate currently falls and what they could plan to plant next should they see a climate shift. Jones created the climate chart from existing places where varieties were already popular, so some could argue that it should be used as a description of the status quo, not a guide to what is possible.

Alston spots the problem with matching grapes with climates purely on scientific merit. "This big problem for wine is that when you've created a collective reputation with AVAs for producing super premium Cabernet Sauvignon – that's hard to get around. When the climate makes it hard to do Cabernet Sauvignon, you're not going to shift to some Spanish variety very quickly."[24] Napa growers know their customers like them making Cabernet. Those customers might not like their version of Tempranillo, a warmer climate grape, and they might not like Tempranillo at all.

It may make sense for wine regions without a long history of growing to change grape varieties, but it's harder to branch out when regional identity is tied to a specific family of varieties, and when the consumers must muddle through a long transition period. Indeed, some regions specifically forbid new varieties. In Burgundy, where Pinot Noir and Chardonnay go back centuries, it's hard to imagine, say, Syrah being grown, and it's nearly impossible to imagine the region retaining the same sky-high prices with another grape. This transition would precipitate an identity crisis, acting as a permanent disincentive to adapt.

For many consumers, switching away from their favorite variety from their favorite region is like being told to stop following their favorite sports team. The Chicago Cubs held the longest World Series drought in history at 107 years without winning. If they could keep devoted fans for over a century despite never being the best, could a wine region that is past its climatic prime retain its fans for the chance that once in 100 years, it might achieve a vintage reminiscent of its heyday? How devoted can wine fans be? For wine growers, betting that their fans will love them playing the same game and coming up short is a better gamble than changing who they are. Are the adaptive possibilities in farming enough to overcome the pressures of climate change and continue making wine that consumers know and love?

* * *

There is a suite of responses to a warming climate, from the ingeniously simple to the devilishly expensive. Some of the simplest are adjustments to the vine canopy (angling or spreading the leaves to shade the grapes), adjusting grapevine height to avoid solar radiation from rocky soils, replanting with more drought-tolerant rootstocks or reorienting rows to lessen hot afternoon sun. Other strategies include shade cloth or misting with water, though these may be expensive or water-intensive. Some are proposing planting trees nearby to cool the ground, though the impact of this is difficult to gauge.

Despite growers making these changes, it's unclear whether it's enough to maintain traditional wine profiles. Growers can adjust their farming and pick grapes earlier to achieve lower alcohols and pHs and higher acids, but the worry still exists that other flavor and aroma compounds will change. Kees van Leeuwen observes, "I'm very, very, very convinced that aromatic ripeness, much more than phenolic ripeness, is the key to understanding wine typicity."[25] Given the complexity and mystery of how climate shapes the myriad variables that define a wine, those defending the idea that historic regions will not change have their work cut out for them.

One of the more aggressive strategies is to change which plots the best wine comes from. In northern Italy, south of the Alps, Piedmont is questioning how to maintain quality in the face of a changing climate. Historically, the south-facing hills were the most prized because they were exposed to the sun and able to ripen the Nebbiolo grape. Now, some growers in hot years are leaving the southern-exposed fruit for other wines and harvesting the southwest and southeast sections for their best wines because those exposures better protect from the heat. In regions like Piedmont where the rules allow this flexibility, they can still make the best wine possible each vintage, though whether the product will resemble years past is still an open question.

In Burgundy, where the grapes grown are limited by law and the *grand cru* sites are fixed in place, the question emerges as to whether those sites are making the same style of wines as they have historically. For those arguing that soil is the dominant justification for *grand cru* status, or for any great site around the world, the prospect of climate change is less alarming. For those who are convinced that climate is the primary mover and shaker of terroir expression, then climate change is problematic at best and existentially damning at worst.

For those who take climate seriously as a primary factor of site expression, even if *grand cru* sites were to adapt, the question arises whether to carry on legally enshrining them as hallowed ground. Perhaps a site with similar soil structure in a slightly cooler place in the hands of a talented vigneron is capable of similar quality. Growers looking to maintain the grandness of their *crus* can't play the Piedmontese game of shifting site – they need another tool.

* * *

Not far away, a South African researcher at the École Supérieure des Agricultures in Angers, in the Loire region of France, is considering what growers might be able to do to adapt. Having visited France for school, Etienne Neethling fell in love, married, and settled permanently into family life and a research career. He is one of the researchers sounding the alarm on climate change's effect on regional identity, with altered ripening patterns resulting in distinctly different flavors. He cites the example of the Loire, the mean temperature of which, in the last twenty years, has been equivalent to the mean average temperature in the 1950s and 1960s of Bordeaux, which is 180 miles (290 kilometers) to the south of Angers.[26]

He is not a catastrophist, though, and his optimistic counterargument to regional identity crises rests on the years of research he has done on vine clones. "Most of the commercial clones were selected in the seventies and eighties at a time in France when the weather was cold; we wanted to have high yields, we wanted to have high sugar – low acidity. And today, if you look at those criteria of selection, it's actually the opposite that we're looking for."[27] Some of the clones Neethling is studying ripen upwards of three weeks later than their early ripening counterparts currently planted in France.

The crux of Neethling's argument rests on two pillars. Firstly, accepting the premise that more delicate aromas develop in wines that ripen later in the season; Neethling thinks he can recapture some of the flavor compounds that are supposedly being lost. Secondly, by proposing that vintners plant a selection of different clones in one plot, he thinks that the diversity of clones will buffer against the various extreme weather events that will hit vineyards. He uses the example of growers who plant late-ripening clones but then get a cold year – the resulting wine may be too lean and acidic. Better to diversify and have some clones for every seasonal scenario, resulting in a more complex, resilient wine. This is catnip to wine tastemakers who worship at the altar of complexity. Neethling knows how to present a convincing case.

The tension behind Neethling's premise is that a part of what is classically described as terroir actually comes from the purposeful selection of vine types that imbue wine with their own inherent flavor. Some might argue that these vine selections are not important relative to the effects of soil, but others contend that the effects are quite noticeable. In parts of the world where clonal selections are bottled and marketed as such, this effect is clear to see.

Whether Neethling's approach is successful will take some time to become clear. Even if ripening in line with "the old days," some clonal change will shift taste profiles, making comparisons to wines from the previous generations difficult. Wine style isn't completely fixed anyway, even in heavily codified regions. "The moment we moved from massal selection in the fifties to clonal selection in the seventies it definitely brought a change in typicity, for sure, but maybe at the time they wanted this typicity,"[28] says Neethling

Clonal change is just one way that regional typicity can change over time. "The question of maintaining typicity is so complex because we also make wine that evolves with consumers' tastes and consumers' preferences,"[29] Neethling states. Certain wine critics lavishing particular wines with praise may inspire other producers to replicate that style, slowly shifting the typical profile of an entire region. Evolving consumer preference, producer inclination, and production advances in the cellar and vineyard can also lead to changes in typicity.

In this sense, Burgundy, or any place with entrenched interests in classified sites, can defend stylistic shifts by claiming that change over time is a normal part of their culture. What makes a great wine region is not just the style du jour, but the culture, the stories, the people, and its journey of constantly re-examining and recreating its identity. If climate change incidentally lowers some acids and softens some tannins, this is missing the point. The value of a lauded wine region lies in its persona as much as its products.

This argument may appeal to the reflective consumer who is willing to entertain these shifts, but for wine drinkers who fell in love with a particular wine style born of a specific clonal expression only made possible in a particular type of vintage that, through climate shifts, is becoming less and less frequent, this is poor comfort. So what if a wine region is full of interesting people working hard to preserve their livelihood – if the hierarchy of vineyards is built on taste, and that top vineyard no longer tastes the best, why not follow a new group of people discovering what their land can offer.

Neethling makes the argument that fidelity to style ought to be viewed less dogmatically. "My sister and myself, we look similar because you can see there's a family resemblance, but our personality is different. And I think that is where the concept of typicity today has evolved towards a typicity that's plural and no longer singular,"[30] he reflects. With the impact of climate change, how long will it be until certain wines no longer resemble the rest of their regional family?

* * *

Northwest of the Loire, in Brittany, a French academic who did her doctoral research in South Africa adds another layer of complexity to the equation calculating how the prominent wine regions of the world will evolve. Valérie Bonnardot studied the climate of South Africa for eight years, looking into the cooling effect that the coastal breeze had on grape growing there. "I found that [breeze] could be recorded quite, quite far inland, but the impact on temperature and humidity was rapidly stopped due to the complex terrain," she observes.[31]

Bonnardot is quick to point out that coastal breeze manifests different conditions for vines around the world. In South Africa and Uruguay the ocean breeze brings in cool air, helping to moderate daytime temperature highs that are felt more intensely further inland, but in Brittany, where Bonnardot teaches now, she notes that since it's already cool, the breeze serves to help decrease humidity, lowering mildew pressure for vines. Though all vinous regions around the world are heating up, she points out, "The coastal region is a way to face climate change or to avoid the extreme heat of the day, especially during the ripening period."[32]

Noting that climate change has provided benefits to northern regions such as Champagne and Alsace, she turns her attention to Brittany, which used to have vines in the 1800s, went for a long period without them, and only began replanting them in 2019. Of all the regions in France, Brittany's mean average temperature has risen the least, raising questions about the future of vine production and which other regions around the world might be more and less affected. If some regions are more naturally protected by cooling factors like coastal air or high elevation, vintners there may not need to adapt as quickly as in other regions.

The complexity of replanting vines in Brittany is a microcosm of what all emerging wine regions will face. Some might argue that shifts of mean average temperature predetermine vinous greatness, but critics might argue that other elements matter as well – rainfall patterns, hours of daylight, and know-how, not to mention the element that winos love to love, the soil. In the case of Brittany, Bonnardot notes that as a whole, "the soil is not the best," clarifying that growers have had to look for the rarer pockets of schist or other suitable soil.[33] This is partly why the wine growers of Great Britain are so happy to have found Kimmeridgian soils in their backyard – the closer their conditions are to Champagne, in soil as well as climate, the easier it is to market their wines.

Veteran wine regions can attempt to rest their defense in part on these terroir-as-soil premises and might find evidence to support their argument in surprising places. The Judgment of Paris is an interesting case study in the possibility of an underdog region toppling the dominant wines. In 1976 some wines from California famously came first in a blind tasting against some of the most prominent wine regions in France. The climate of the greater Bay Area of California was notably different from that of both its Bordelais and Burgundian counterparts. The fact that these supposedly distinct climates confused the judges belies the idea that the regions are as unique as some argue. Many in blind tasting celebrate and focus on their success in identifying wines from the right region, but some might argue that the very fact that it is difficult proves the capacity of different regions to create a similar product, and therefore proves that regions can be stylistically resilient in the face of a warming planet.

* * *

A German economist named Karl Storchmann, working at New York University, has been trying to shine a light on some of the observable effects on wine as a result of climate change. As editor of the *Journal of Wine Economics* and executive director and vice president of the American Association of Wine Economists, he commands a grasp on arcane wine data that borders on the absurd.

To understand the effect climate change is having on markets, Storchmann is studying Prussian tax collectors of the nineteenth century, attempting to find out how vineyards were valued at the time. Referencing the 1869 tax classification of vineyards, he notes that the best way to understand the value of a wine region is not the current price of a bottle, but the value of the land. Current wine prices can be affected by passing fads or past glory, but land prices reflect not only the money a grower can make now, but the expectation of long-term returns from sales of their wines. In short, land values contain within them multitudes of other data all working towards predicting what the wine from that place can do in the open market.

Storchmann is expecting more research on the topic soon, but theorizes in the meantime how regional valuation is changing: "Languedoc is hot and the price of land has gone down like crazy. So that is in the south … Champagne still has good profits, but the price of land has stopped growing. I think it reached its peak in 2010. Since then it's been relatively flat, which to me is like the market's forecast. Since the price of land looks into the future, I think Champagne has reached its peak."[34] Some can argue that this data is proxy evidence to help determine which regions are coping with climate change and which regions are failing. If repeated heatwaves are stopping people from getting grapes that justify going into a premium bottle, at some point that lack of ability to make a good product will be reflected in land prices.

Storchmann acknowledges that land prices are not a perfect proxy for objective wine value. "It's fashion. China now has crashed absolutely down [sales dropped off], which drags down the prices of Bordeaux wine, and probably also land."[35] The fashionableness of wine regions affects emerging regions, too. "In the UK there's also a lot of marketing … In Patagonia, not so much."[36] Given this unevenness of marketing terrain, there are clearly other factors dictating the long-term stability of emerging regions emboldened by climate change.

* * *

A final question raised by climate change is whether vintners have any power or obligation to fight climate change. Some wineries espouse the benefits of their soil practices, which they claim allow them to sequester carbon. Others have built solar arrays, recycle their water, and have changed their packaging, amongst other practices. Sometimes the collective impact of farming is used as a moral imperative for vintners, who as part of the world of agriculture, it is claimed, have a responsibility to step up.

Given the relatively minuscule effect the wine industry has on climate change relative to most other industries, there is an argument that these gestures are more for marketing than to create any real impact. Critics can point out the irony of a producer employing meticulous environmental precision in a vineyard, only to bottle a product in heavy, relatively inefficient and energy-intensive small containers, send it around the world, and fly around the world promoting it. The level of hypocrisy, some might claim, is quite high. Some serious environmentalists might challenge those in the wine world that if they cared about the environment they could stop altogether and return their vineyards to forests, which would do a much better job at carbon sequestration than any vineyard practice.

While some might be persuaded by this type of argument, others might view stopping the capitalist machine as unrealistic and not helpful. The better path, they say, is to try to balance human wants with attainable environmental goals. Even the smallest ecological effects matter and the only way forward is to foster this attitude across industries that all must do their part. Given that wine is one of the more visible and sexy agricultural endeavors that tourists actually want to see, some can argue that even if the environmental effects might be small, the example set by the wine industry has an outsize impact. Practicality and idealism continue to clash.

The twin questions more immediately affecting the wine consumer are whether existing wine regions and vineyards can (and should) continue to be sustainably farmed and whether the wines can continue to command respect. Part of the reason this debate remains mysterious is that climate change continues to progress at an uncertain pace; it's unclear when and how quickly adaptation will need to take place. Given the incentives for many vintners to preserve the status quo for as long as possible, it is also unclear how many environmentally beneficial changes are currently possible but aren't being discussed. Since adaptation is not a big selling point for most wineries, it's often publicly addressed with simple platitudes about sustainability before marketers revert back to the usual selling points.

There are still a number of practitioners in the industry who regard climate change as an overblown concern. Though data suggests that the climate has changed somewhat, the fears are exaggerated, this group argues. And even if it is a long-term, serious threat to the planet, grapevines are resilient, they argue, farming practices make a huge difference, and all the cultural and intellectual know-how can play a large role in ensuring that babied vines turn out amazing fruit. New regions might spring up, but they are in for extreme weather at the poles too, and it's nearly impossible to uproot all the generations of savoir faire to a new place and start from scratch. And yet, this move seems to be in motion, and the wines have entered the world stage.

The fact that Tasmania, Patagonia, and the United Kingdom, to name a few of the newer entrants, are making wine and gaining investment can be construed as evidence to support those who believe the pendulum may be swinging to new terroirs. Blind tasting's value will grow as entrants and old hands seek to test and retest assumptions. Vintners in new wine regions can exchange information and spread the word in the same way that other regions have done in the past. And environmentalists will continue asking hard questions about viticulture's sustainability around the world, even if the industry can only effect so much change on its own. In this sense, every new vintage from every wine region, drunk in restaurants, wine bars, and living rooms around the world is an opportunity to assess whether the glass and its origin are worth fighting for.

6
Aesthetic theories of quality: what can we really taste?

"Truth is disputable; not taste."

David Hume, *An Enquiry Concerning the Principles of Morals*

When music fans hear "Bad Romance" it's simple pop trivia to know that Lady Gaga is the force behind it. When art lovers see the painting, *A Sunday Afternoon on the Island of La Grande Jatte*, most know that Georges Seurat is responsible. And faced with a sample of writing that references Frodo and the ring, readers know they are holding a book by J. R. R. Tolkien.

In so many fields our senses are infrequently tested this way and at least for the famous examples we can easily determine the origin of the work in front of us. With wine it is less clear. Tasting a wine blind, without the biases of knowing the creative force behind it, exposes wine and other beverages to unvarnished critical appraisal. The fact that blind tasting can be so easily and quickly organized ensures that wine is continually reappraised and placed under objective scrutiny.

The Paris Wine Tasting of 1976 (aka Judgment of Paris), in which influential French judges compared French and Californian wines and ranked them, is perhaps the most historically significant of these tastings because, unexpectedly, wines from then little-known Napa and Sonoma came first. The countless blind tastings comparing all sorts of wines from around the world and the attempt to rank them on a hierarchical scale has defined much of wine criticism and the culture of wine today. The underlying premise holding up this system is that regardless of stylistic changes and different flavors, a universal idea of quality can exist.

As time went on, some began to question the central assumption – how could it be that people with so many different tastes in food could coalesce around a linear ordering of wine? And if different people have different preferences and senses of taste, what's the point of attempting to blind taste wines to assess quality to begin with? From this perspective, we gain nothing from the blind scoring of wines – maybe a wine could be described, maybe a wine's history could be discussed, but our different taste appreciations make scoring unhelpful at best.

These stances are at opposite ends of the argument, but many of those who find either view too extreme would still debate the importance of blind ranking, and the ability of anyone drinking or reviewing to taste consistently over time. To what degree can we even reliably recommend wines to our friends, or trust our own palates?

* * *

Born in South Africa, Hildegarde Heymann decided to become a winemaker before she had even tasted wine. She settled in California in the late 1970s when the wine scene was still rugged but in the ascendant. Rather than becoming a winemaker, she fell for the academic work of sensory science, training under Anne Noble, the creator of the wine flavor wheel. She now holds the position of distinguished professor of viticulture and enology at UC Davis, focusing her research on sensory science, and is the co-author of *Sensory Evaluation of Foods: Principles and Practices*. Recounting the post-Prohibition history of wine in the state, she says, "There was a lot of flawed wine being made and so the twenty-point scorecard was essentially created to eliminate those wines from the marketplace. Now, today, most of the problems on that score sheet don't happen anymore … most wines would probably score 18, 19, 20 – so it's a totally irrelevant scale."[1] What Dr. Heymann is referring to as flaws include a litany of aromas such as *Brettanomyces*, or Brett (can smell like barnyard or Band-Aid), oxidation, mousiness (the floor of a dirty mouse cage), ropiness, ethyl acetate (smells like nail polish remover), and cork taint, to name a few. These sorts of issues often arose due to poor winery practices, but as wineries came into increasing competition with one another, they fought to improve cleanliness and general quality. This school of thought suggests that while deliciousness may be hard to measure and agree on, a minimum barrier to entry is the absence of faults. As Brillat-Savarin said in 1825, "man is much more sensitive to pain than to pleasure."[2]

Flaws vary in type and severity, however. Just about everyone agrees that cork taint or smoke taint is bad, but oxidation, Brett, ethyl acetate, and most recently, mousiness, for example, have garnered more mixed opinions. Idealism in wine rarely stagnates, and the current countermovement in taste has embraced some of these previously frowned-upon characteristics. After the scientific quality improvement movements of the nineteenth and twentieth centuries, wine consumers now live in a dreamscape of limitless, squeaky-clean bottles, but the great irony is that some have criticized the alleged sameness of wine and have advocated that wineries retain some level of imperfection. Perfection through imperfection is a very different theory of quality that would preclude the old UC Davis scale.

This movement has become quite widespread, challenging the absence-of-faults theory around the globe. At Le Bernardin, a three-star Michelin restaurant in Manhattan, the question, "What do you recommend?" has drawn the response, "What do you think of mousiness?" said in the tone of voice that invites acceptance. The juxtaposition of a previously untouchable aroma in a space reserved for treating food as holy illuminates just how high-up this movement has reached. If these aromas are supposed to be inherently offensive, how can they have clawed their way back from oblivion?

* * *

Leigh Francis, a PhD in wine chemistry, ran sensory science tests at the Australian Wine Research Institute (AWRI) from the late 1980s up until 2023. Founded in 1955, AWRI undertakes research trials with the goal of helping the Australian wine industry, and Francis has been one of the giants of sensory science in the country. Despite his contributions to the field, he has maintained a quiet presence in the wine world: he speaks softly but in his research trials he carries a big sample size. Discussing the appeal of wine faults, he notes, "When you test people blind, generally ordinary wine consumers don't appreciate any of those faulty sort of characters. There are very few … You're looking to see if there's a subgroup of people who really do appreciate that flavor, and generally it's not the case."[3]

The implications of Francis's assessment are a blow against the "all wine is subjective" school of thought. He acknowledges some consumers appreciate wines with volatile acidity in small quantities, but for the most part he points to the limits of asserting that there are no universal truths in taste. Depending on the compound, like trichloroanisole, one of the causes of cork taint, some might not be able to detect it, but about wine faults in general he concludes: "The various tests we've done with various consumers over many years – consumers from different backgrounds and different countries to some extent – we don't see that there's an appreciation."[4]

* * *

Stephen Brook, a British wine writer and critic, acknowledges the schism in quality adjudication, where intelligent minds and experienced tongues may disagree on what level of fault is acceptable in a wine. "I'm of the school that finds a lot of so-called wine faults acceptable in modest doses, such as modest Brett or VA [volatile acidity], but obviously taken to excess, it's not a good thing."[5] From this centrist position, two questions emerge: why is it that some appreciate flaws in small doses to begin with, and what defines a small dose?

Part of the theory behind quality movements has been the central idea that part of what defines a flaw is the accidental nature of it, but in a marketplace where most wine is technically flawless, perhaps the few with small flaws stand out. In a lineup of 20 wines, if one flawed wine makes the rest taste relatively samey, its uniqueness may draw the taster's focus, fostering a greater sense of appreciation.

Those paying attention to Leigh Francis's work and other blind tasting trials might suggest that this is more of a trick of focus and differentiation than of inherently good taste, but winemakers could argue that by intentionally making an unexpected wine they are reframing the drinker's focus, drawing attention to complexity and nuance and creating pleasure from the mental experience as much as from the wine itself. In that sense, a flaw's ability to draw attention is circumstantial – it may work for someone surrounded by unblemished wines, but in the context of the eighteenth century where faulty aromas were commonplace, all the flaw stood for was the banality of imperfect winemaking.

Another theory is that a slight imperfection helps humanize something, which could explain why these wines fare better when not tasted in an analytical, laboratory blind tasting. It's hard to appreciate the humanity of something in a clinical lab setting where all ties to humanity are cut off. In this sense, the flaw can frame the perfection, making us appreciate it more. When an artist intentionally leaves a brushstroke visible for the viewer, they are purposefully breaking the idea of the painting as reality, intending that the viewer appreciates the humanity and heightened beauty of the piece.

The question still stands though: once society is past the novelty of appreciating the artistic symbolism behind the wine, how much of the flaw can be tolerated before the balance is tipped towards disgust? Stephen Brook recounts an experience of this sort of disagreement: "I've judged a lot in Australia and it's a rather terrifying experience because I remember there was one winemaker there who was an experienced judge, and I was with her and she found that about one third of the wines that we were tasting were flawed – invariably Brett. I just, I just didn't see it."[6] This viewpoint perhaps implies more subjectivism in the wine world than the strict laboratory tastings might suggest.

* * *

Part of what permits such rigorous debate about wine faults is that it's possible to measure their presence by chemical analysis. Once flaws have been removed from the picture, the quality debate becomes more complex, first over the qualities that make a wine good, and second over the number of people who agree.

One of the first theories of wine appreciation is to pursue the types of characteristics that might not be classically defined as faults but are argued to be perceptually antagonistic in some way. Leigh Francis explains, "Consumers know what they don't like and they will respond strongly to things they don't like, and if a wine is harsh, has a lot of tannin, fairly strong acid – they often won't like it as much as a wine that is less harsh, less tannin, less acid. And sometimes that can be achieved by having a slightly sweet wine."[7] Bitterness, alcohol level, and particularly potent unripe aromas are other aspects of quality that commonly arise in discussion.

For many, augmenting the argument that soft, approachable wines appeal to people was a study done with Chinese consumers comparing wines from all over the world. Wes Pearson, another researcher at AWRI, who happens to also make wine and has judged competitions, recounts how participants were presented with a selection of international wines without knowing the country of origin and then were instructed to re-taste wines once the countries had been revealed. "They loved the fruity Australian wine. That was their preference. As soon as you showed them the label, it was the least preferred and they loved the French wine."[8]

* * *

There is a theory of taste backed up by evolutionary biology that supports the idea that softer and fruitier wines are more pleasurable. Humans evolved to dislike bitterness because bitterness is often found in toxic substances. Bitter tannins are believed to have developed to protect plants from predation. Conversely, fruity aromas and alcohol are indicators of ripeness that help signal that food is ready for consumption. The more nuanced view of this biological perspective is that some acid, tannin, and even bitterness is allowable in a high-quality wine so long as it is not strong enough to dominate the entire profile of the wine. Overall, this theory of positive wine quality can be summarized as follows: people tend to like the things that historically kept them alive.

The premise that fruity, approachable wines are desirable and that desire defines quality is an idea that faces more than a little criticism, undoubtedly from within Australia as well. Popularity does not define refinement, some might counter. First, there is the argument that tannic wines might be judged harshly while young but with time will get better. Generally speaking, what makes the tannins more approachable is the very fact that they are softening, so a wine with high tannins might find favour further down the road. The other critique is that this theory can be proven wrong as evidenced by a whole host of wines made with high tannin, high acid, and more savory profiles and they don't seem to be unpopular, and many regard them as being of high quality.

The next tier of the response is the experience argument, an argument that for obvious reasons many professionals in the wine world would have an affinity for. Preference for savory, structured wines with subtle aromas is an acquired taste. As children, we hate bitter vegetables and love sugar and sweets, but when we grow up, we're more likely to appreciate kale and other foods with challenging flavors. We see the same phenomenon of developing tastes in the wine world.

And what's more, differences in human taste perceptions are so common that taking the average of a group is a misleading measure because it ignores the element of unique genetic predetermination in our tastes. "We are all hugely different," Hildegarde Heymann notes. "We all smell differently. We see differently, we taste differently. And I'm not talking about big things like colorblindness; I'm talking about amino acid differences in your receptors that make you entirely different from me."[9] As a sensory scientist herself, Hildegarde is certainly not dismissing the idea that professional sensory panels can collect quality reviews and ensure levels of preference are statistically significant.

* * *

While some implicitly view taste as operating in a vacuum, an interplay of chemistry, taste buds, and smell, others include culture and society in the equation. Stephen Brook, no doubt speaking for many, questions the role his upbringing had in appreciating the wines he does. "Are we too tolerant of our cultural input, as it were? Maybe there are times when we are forgiving of wine styles or wine faults because we grew up with them."[10]

John Prescott, a psychologist and sensory scientist, begins his book, *Taste Matters: Why We Like the Foods We Do*, with the example of *hákarl*, a shark prepared for consumption by burying it in gravel and leaving it to rot.[11] If a culture can appreciate something so viscerally off-putting to an outsider, then what's stopping cultures with highly astringent or oxidized wines from loving these sorts of wine the most?

Research has been done to measure people's appreciation of wines produced in their home regions. The claim that locals always prefer their home town wines was somewhat attenuated by a 2013 blind tasting study showing that while Spanish citizens of Rioja preferred their local wines to those of the Rhône, the same could not be said of drinkers from the Rhône, among whom the results were more finely balanced, giving a slight edge to the Spanish wines.[12] More research is needed to be sure on this issue, but the people pushing for a cultural lens to taste would argue that the differences between the two groups were due to culture and that culture plays a role in determining what wines we like. Those with a less biased view might suggest the Spanish wines were objectively tastier, but this is a cultural bombshell so this sort of conversation rarely takes place in public.

There are genetic differences that play a role in regional comparisons as well. Wes Pearson gives the example of an experiment that tested different ethnic groups to understand their taste comprehension of the bitter compound 6-*n*-propylthiouracil:

> *So we put it on little pieces of paper, and then you just take the paper and you put it on your tongue, and to about a quarter of the population, it just tastes like paper ... 50 percent of the population say, "That's pretty bitter." A quarter of the population say, "That's revolting. That's like I've dissolved two aspirins on my tongue. It is terrible." Those people [the third group] got labeled super tasters ... But what's interesting is when you change ethnic groups. In southeast and northern Asia the group of people that doesn't taste that compound goes from a quarter of the population to two or three percent of the population.*[13]

This is one example from a large body of studies examining taste comparisons between those of different genetic heritages that illustrates the futility of looking for truly objective taste standards for wine.

If people aren't culturally inculcated, can they still move beyond soft, fruity, inoffensive wines into more complex, challenging tastes? Despite the genetic differences in taste discernment, do we share enough in common that it is still worthwhile having a collective conversation on wine quality?

* * *

One of the intriguing tensions at play throughout the debates on what makes a quality wine is the extent to which wine professionals and seasoned tasters align with first-time drinkers. How much more can experienced tasters notice and appreciate relative to casual drinkers or imbibers still on their training wheels, and what are the implications for wine quality?

This matters because regardless of the debates above, the wines that tend to get higher prices, higher scores, and more press tend to get those accolades from professionals. Is wine more like art, in which experts tend to notice more and their previous experiences inform and elevate their viewing? Some might suggest that for wine, as with music, a greater education sometimes allows for greater enjoyment, while others argue that they can be viscerally joyful, and do not require a history of listening or drinking to achieve peak joy. Since wine, like art, has many gatekeepers before the bottle arrives on a restaurant list, the question is how much someone new to wine can trust a sommelier to select a wine that suits her taste.

One person who attempted to bridge this gap is Robin Goldstein, an academic who goes slightly against the grain. At the fifteenth Annual Conference of the American Association of Wine Economists in 2023, he chose to present his writings on the history of food culture in America in the form of a musical called *The War on Pleasure*, which he sang at a piano.

He has organized tastings, which he later compiled into a book, where he asked consumers to blind-taste wines and rank them by how much they liked them. The results showed that for untrained drinkers, there was a slight negative correlation between wine price and wine liking, a finding that did not hold true for the experienced tasters.[14] In other words, as wine prices went up, inexperienced tasters liked the wines a little less and experienced drinkers liked the wines a little more, without knowing the prices of the wines as they made their choices.

This study, along with a follow-up confirmation by the economist Robert Ashton,[15] inadvertently questioned both the value of professional recommendations to beginners and how good amateurs are at identifying quality. Goldstein himself identifies one of the challenges of blind tasting as he reflects on his previous study: "The wines that distinguish themselves most in blind tasting, for example – there tends to be something extreme about them compared to other wines you're comparing them to."[16] This is something that can happen with tasters at all levels when given so many wines that they experience palate fatigue. Wines that stand out in a lineup can be disproportionately liked or disliked when consumers are directed to rank the wines. Perhaps without the prompting of a research team to rank them, more people would have been satisfied, saying the wines were equally good, just different, but that is critical conjecture. Or perhaps consumers are prompted by the base pleasure aspects identified by Leigh Francis.

Part of Goldstein's thinking in his study was to test and draw attention to what he viewed as the snobbishness of the wine world. "I like to talk about the difference between geeks and snobs," he says, reflecting on his trial. "To me, like, geeks and snobs may both know a lot about the product and love to geek out about it, but snobs are the ones who look down on other people for their tastes."[17] In Goldstein's telling, taste perceptions are different enough to justify not obsessively focusing on rankings.

One of the criticisms of determining wine quality via inexperienced drinkers on sensory panels is that while there might be a statistically significant finding, some experienced tasters think they might be selecting what they like in a less rigorous and therefore possibly more random pattern. An experienced taster might taste rough tannins, but know that the wine will soften in the next few years, so rate it higher than an amateur. An experienced taster might know to spit the wine between drinks, and have more sober judgments. A more experienced taster might have grown more bored of some of the flavors of cheap vanilla-tasting oak on entry level wines.

In all these cases, the amateur may eventually agree with the expert, they just don't see it in the moment. For those who follow this critique, a comparison they might use would be to ask whether it's appropriate for people who eat mostly fast food to be the judges for fine dining restaurants. Though risking cultural elitism, the question remains over what the divide is between these two groups.

Lastly, perhaps the wine industry understands that people's palates evolve as they drink more and they are correctly making entry level wine for entry level palates but changing their wines to anticipate the different sorts of flavors that more experienced tasters will like. They likely anticipate that most people drinking these more expensive wines have already gone on a wine journey and have grown to appreciate those tastes. This still begs the question of whether an entry level drinker should splurge on an expensive bottle of wine or trust an expert taster. Does the amateur taster notice as much?

* * *

To understand how good students of wine are at tasting, it's helpful to stop and examine one of the most discussed papers on taste. A young French PhD student and winemaker, Frédéric Brochet, was interested in color in relation to how humans think. In his 2001 paper, he wrote, "The classic example of behavior analysis is the Stroop test, in which it can be observed that red written in red is read more quickly than blue written in yellow."[18] Could this cognitive quirk affect how we perceive wine?

Another motivator for Brochet was the price hierarchies in French wine. He had been making wine in Poitiers and was frustrated with the lack of appreciation for what he estimated to be a perfectly good wine. "We had a Pinot Noir, which was really – and is still – world class standout. But no one believed in it because people in France would say, 'Where does it come from?' 'Oh. It's good for Poitiers, but it's – you know … How much do you sell it for? Ten euros? Oh gosh. I'll pay two euros for that because it's only a Poitiers region wine."[19] Brochet was an excellent chemistry student and had determined that the wine was analytically similar to many from Burgundy, so he set up a study to see how much attention drinkers were paying to what was in their glass when making a judgment.

Brochet analyzed the wine reviews of four wine publications, identifying the words generally associated with red descriptions and white descriptions. He then began his experiment, opting, as many researchers do, to use the guinea pigs of the academic world as his test subjects: undergraduate students. In this case, there were 54 of them, all studying enology at the University of Bordeaux. Brochet first had them describe a red and a white Bordeaux wine, noting which words they generally used to describe reds and which were generally used to describe whites. For example, words the students wrote down when describing the white wine (but not the red) included floral, honey, apple, pear, and butter, to name a few. Examples of terms students used to describe the red Bordeaux wine included blackcurrant, raspberry, cherry, spice, animal, and vanilla.

A week later, Brochet summoned the same group of undergrads back to the lab, where he had laid his research trap. The students arrived to find two glasses appearing much the same as the previous week, one white and one red. This time, however, Brochet had put the same white wine in both glasses, adding an odorless and tasteless red dye to one of the glasses. He gave each taster the descriptive terms that they had used the previous week and asked them to describe the wines using either the words on the list or any new terms that they deemed appropriate.

Reviewing the details of how this study was set up is important, because the results would go on to shock the wine world. When analyzing the descriptions of the wines, Brochet found that students had used the white wine descriptors for the un-dyed wine and the red wine descriptors for the same white wine dyed red.

Some journalists jumped on the study as proof that wine tasting was demonstrably bullshit, with a *Guardian* headline titled "Wine-tasting: it's junk science" citing Brochet's work amongst others to justify the claim. Some, opining on how easily the students turned to the wrong descriptor, suggested that this proved that the ability to blind taste was only a tiny element in how wines are actually judged in real life. They argued that psychology matters more than taste.

Others dismissed the study, attempting to poke holes in the methodology, and defending the concept of objective taste. After all, should you really reassess your entire understanding of how humans perceive wine based on what a number of undergrads did once? Expectation and direction plays a leading role in this drama. If the students had not been recently prompted to come up with generic red and white descriptors, perhaps more of them would have used a broader range of vocabulary? By giving the students those words, couldn't the students infer that the researchers thought they would be useful for the tasting? And why not apply them to the reds and whites like they did the previous week?

And perhaps effort plays a role as well. One imagines an overworked undergraduate student, their thoughts focused more on getting quickly through the tasting to get out and move on to the next thing. If you're given a red and white glass and asked to describe them with recent vocabulary, it might be tempting to give the quick answer without thinking very deeply. In the same way that students asked to look at a film of basketball players bouncing a ball missed the gorilla, these students might still be able to taste well, they just took a shortcut that usually works without thinking they needed to pay close attention.[20]

Blind tasters everywhere would be wise to take note that the color in the glass may bias their judgments. This is particularly tricky because anyone who has ever taken a wine tasting class will know that the first thing the instructor does is ask the class to resist sniffing or sipping the wine, but instead to look at the color.

We're taught that this is a clue that we should use in assessing wine. If a white wine is more golden or a red wine is fading with a brown tinge around the edge, then we are urged to consider that the wine might be old. Certain tints of color, for example, a purplish hue, are meant to lead us towards Gamay or Malbec. The insinuation that we should ignore this chromatic evidence is akin to telling a detective at a murder scene to ignore the drops of blood leading to the closet.

Unsurprisingly, researchers and civilians alike have thought to run experiments on distinguishing white and red wines since as early as the 1980s. It is likely that people experimented casually with this proposition before professionalized studies began to appear in journals. When prompted to guess red or white in a literally blind setting (or at very least with the wine in a black glass, obscuring the color), the success rate depends on the wine. A very tannic red is harder to confuse for a white than a light red.

* * *

One researcher who has done further analysis on the degree of difference between professional and amateur rankings is Dr Qian Janice Wang MW. Now at the University of Copenhagen, Wang was a graduate student at Oxford and competed against Cambridge on the blind tasting team. She was also a researcher, tracking the preferences of her teammates as they blind-tasted through wines, looking for changes in which wines they claimed to like as they grew from novice to experienced. She found that the students who tasted wine over a longer period of study liked wines with higher acidity and alcohol, and less oaky influence.[21] Their preferences also lined up more with price hierarchy than when they were untrained.

One question to ask is to what extent these drinkers changed their preferences based on their own blank-slate preferences, and to what extent those changes were formed based on biases received from their trainers. Wang comments, "Our coach has a very elegant, austere taste, and I think she has single handedly shaped the taste of generations of wine tasters. So it's a learned behavior. I'm a hundred percent sure."[22] One interpretation of the results is that, as tasters train, their preferences evolve independently to appreciate new aspects of wine in a fairly instinctual, natural way. Another interpretation is that their preferences were shaped by their coach. Whether our environment or our natural instincts play the most powerful part is the ultimate question of quality.

This question returns to the original premise – are taste preferences random or is there any unifying aesthetic theory of wine that can make different people agree on what tastes good? The most common idea for a theory of universal quality is the idea of balance. The underlying idea behind balance is that none of the structural elements of the wine stand out. The wine isn't overly alcoholic, overly acidic, overly tannic – none of the elements is more pronounced than the others and the wine is a cohesive whole. Dr. Heymann attempts to describe it: "I cannot find a way of describing it objectively using sensory terms. It's not acidic, it's not astringent, it's just this smooth ball. And my brain is going, oh, this is yummy."[23]

Since balance relates to the structural elements of wine chemistry, a criticism of balance presents itself. Some wines, like Gewürztraminer, have incredibly low acid, while other wines, like Riesling, are famous for their high acidity. In red wines, Nebbiolo has very high tannin while Pinot Noir is much more lacking in this area. If an aesthetic theory leads to an ideal of perfect chemical balance, then some wine varieties would be jettisoned from the conversation about what the best wines in the world might be. When discussing niche or bulk varieties many in the wine community might make an argument that there is something about the chemical balance of these wines that explains why they are not as popular. When discussing Riesling or Nebbiolo, some, but fewer would make this claim. Even within the arena of balance, natural preferences likely allow for the debate about ideal aesthetic quality to continue.

Part of what seems to allow the same drinker to accept as balanced two wines with seemingly opposite chemical make-up is the knowledge that "for the type," the balance is correct. If someone were expecting a Riesling, but instead had the low acid and high pH more typical of a Gewürztraminer, they might spit it out. But knowing what to expect allows them to appreciate it more. Professional tasters tend to have more of these expectations, and many judge wines based on the typicity of their varietal character, placing a premium on this. Amateur tasters might push back, suggesting that what a variety normally tastes like should have no bearing on whether it is deemed to be good or not. The communication question of whether a universal ideal is being judged or a variety is being judged for its historical character makes the conversation more tricky.

In addition to balance, the Wine and Spirits Education Trust (WSET) lists length, intensity, and complexity as part of their key elements for quality, using the acronym BLIC. Part of the reason that length and intensity are appreciated is down to history: in the past, cheap wines were watered down to create more volume. It was natural to value intensity and length because it was the polar opposite of this cheap winemaking approach. In the modern era, some might want to add more nuance to this. For an inoffensive wine, these attributes might be positive, but in the case of a wine with bitter or other negative aspects, the drinker might want there to be less length and intensity. It's clear then that these attributes require a base level of deliciousness before they can clearly be placed in the positive attribute column.

Complexity is often proved to be a part of quality by proof that its antonym is decidedly not good: monolithic things get tiring. Musical critics move on from "Three Blind Mice" for the same reason that wine critics move on from bland wines. Assuming that a wine has no egregious faults and is well balanced, should complex wines be viewed as higher quality than those with simpler or more banal flavors? Most in the wine community answer unquestionably in the affirmative, though there are undoubtedly differences in how much to rely on complexity as an arbiter of quality. Some might even suggest that complexity can actually make a wine worse if all the aspects of wine contributing to complexity are negative.

Part of the case for complexity as a determinant of quality is that it helps draw our attention making the drinker want to consider the wine more closely. Peter de Bolla, a Professor of Cultural History and Aesthetics at King's College, Cambridge, also runs the wine program at the college, overseeing a massive cellar, part of which is stored underneath the College's immense, early nineteenth century dining hall. It's not always the case that someone in a wine buying position is so literate in aesthetic theories, so he is perhaps uniquely qualified to weigh in on the issue. As he explains complexity, its beauty lies within its ability to command and hold attention:

And so it's the attention, it's the cessation of attention or the prolongation of attention. And that's true of all artworks. I'm going to Paris in a couple of days to see a huge Rothko exhibition in Paris and one of the reasons why I like and value and think that the paintings that Rothko made are so incredibly beautiful is because they require very long attentive spans in order to get some sense of what the paintings are doing. So that extension of one's attending to the object is one of the main drivers of aesthetic pleasure. And that is true also of wine.[24]

* * *

How much to value complexity, balance, length, intensity, level of faults, level of ripeness, and all the other factors is what makes the aesthetic judgment of wines so difficult. One 2008 paper from the *Journal of Wine Economics* set out to test the reliability of wine judges at a California wine fair. The judges were given the same wine multiple times to measure how consistent they were. The paper concluded, "About 10 percent of the judges were able to replicate their score within a single medal group. Another 10 percent, on occasion, scored the same wine Bronze to Gold. Judges tend to be more consistent in what they don't like than what they do."[25]

This research has been used to criticize reviewers in the wine world, who might not be as capable of infallible taste as some might have assumed. At its worst, the implicit claim is that ideas of quality are so vague that it is not even worth attempting to judge them. Others might defend professional wine judges, suggesting that a state wine fair is not the best place to find the high caliber judges or to limit the number of wines tasted to a reasonable number. A more scientific environment with a more trained panel could help, these wine critic defenders would argue. Still, an amateur taster might look at this and ask what it means for their ability to have consistent favorite wines if relatively more experienced judges struggle to achieve the same consistency.

One possible adjustment is to break apart rankings into separate categories. This begs the question of whether one ranking system can be used to compare wines as dissimilar as rosé from Provence and Tanat, the highly tannic red wine commonly from Uruguay. One of the criticisms of a universal ranking system for all wines is that it has left rosé wines to rarely achieve the level of points that other wines get as a matter of course. The 100 point system, which in theory has the strength of attempting to create a unified theory of wine quality, can be criticized by those who don't think there is such a thing as one aesthetic theory to bring together different sorts of wines and people.

Stephen Brook defends the role of critical wine assessment: "It's not the role of the wine critic to impose a view. I think we can suggest what we think is a correct view. I don't think we can take it much further than that."[26] If the "correct view" of aesthetic taste is not the goal of all wine critics, then what is, what is it about trained wine tasters that allows them to determine this boundary?

This raises another theory of wine evaluation in which the reviewer takes a less personal stance on taste and asks whether the wine was made in a sound way. If the wine isn't to the personal tastes of the critic, so be it, as long as the winemaker intended to make the wine in that style. This sort of tasting would entail a lot more work on the part of the critic, attempting to understand the winemaker's abilities as well as the quality of the wine. And it also leaves open the question of what happens if a winemaker intends to make a wine that most would regard as objectively bad. Taking these different theories and balancing them seems to be the best approach of many critics, but it leaves open the question of how to weigh these competing aesthetic theories.

Amidst all the attempts to break apart how to rate the quality of a wine, others prefer to speak more poetically about what makes certain wines great. Graziana Grassini is a respected consulting winemaker and a member of the Scientific Committee of the Italian National Organization of Wine Tasters. In 2022 the Minister of Agriculture, Food and Forestry appointed her as the

Vice Chair of the Appellate Tasting Committee of DOCG and DOC wines, where she helps to determine quality and typicity of Italian wines. She recounts asking her legendary mentor, Giacomo Tachis, what a great wine is. "He answered me, closing his eyes as he rocked in his chair: you see, Graziana, a great wine is one that by taking a sip and closing your eyes makes you see the immense."[27]

Given the complexity of rating wines, resorting to poetic language is the answer for many. Still, the deeper questions persist. Because of the difficulty of assessing wine quality do we conclude that all wines have something to offer or is this just milquetoast cultural relativism? What forms our tastes more, the nature of intrinsic taste or the nurture of cultural familiarity and training? The only way to find out is to keep drinking.

7
The value of wine

> *"Art becomes so specialized as to be comprehensible only to artists, and they complain bitterly of public indifference to their work. Competition arises. The wild battle for success becomes more and more material. Small groups who have fought their way to the top of the chaotic world of art and picture-making entrench themselves in the territory they have won. The public, left far behind, looks on bewildered, loses interest and turns away."*
>
> Wassily Kandinsky, *Concerning the Spiritual in Art*

> *"Knowledge creates liking because it creates more meaning."*
>
> Dan Ariely[1]

Nestled between Park Avenue and Lexington Avenue in midtown Manhattan sits the Grill Restaurant. Most guests look up at the glamorous, mid-century modern fixtures adorning its high ceilings, but those who also pick up the wine list and scan all the way to the bottom will find a bottle of wine for sale for $300,000. Regardless of how often, or if ever, the wine is ordered, the existence of a bottle on a restaurant list for that price begs the question: how did this form of liquified audacity come to be?

The debate over where wine's value originates isn't argued from behind a podium for all to hear, but resides in the menus, publications, journals, and conversations of the wine world. To help understand wine value, there are three key questions to consider.

The first is to what degree and how often wine price and quality are correlated. Some argue that the more expensive the bottle the better tasting the wine, but others disagree and believe wine pricing is irrational, and not helpful for consumers.

Next we must ask, to what extent does the price of wine derive from other non-taste factors such as cultural significance, historical importance, rarity, uniqueness, authenticity, purity, connection to nature, or other ideas that ultimately reside not in the chemistry of the wine, but in the psychological construct of our minds?

At the end of the day, a wine's price is merely a proposal by the producer or the seller of what the value of that wine is, with the hope that the market will validate their claim with a purchase – a financial vote of confidence. The final question for those who don't believe price is correlated to taste or cultural value is how wine should be valued. Is there another way to value wine?

* * *

One reason why the question of whether price correlates with quality has been difficult for academics to answer is the challenge in finding a technical and measurable definition of quality. Kym Anderson, an Australian economist, points out that "In Australia, the average retail price of wine has hardly changed in nominal dollar terms for thirty years, yet the quality of that wine has gone up enormously."[2] The vulgar economic term "increased efficiency" rarely enters refined wine vocabulary, yet there is an argument that the slow, industry-wide improvement of farming and winemaking has counterintuitively lowered the price of good wine.

Anderson points to the classic economic equation of supply and demand to explain why: "The growth in demand until recently, globally, in wine and particularly fine wine, has grown faster than the supply. And so those prices have become stratospheric. So that's the opposite, and it's not that the quality of that wine has increased."[3] In this telling, objective ideas of quality might not have a strong relationship with price because so long as a quality wine is made in a high enough quantity, the demand cannot justify a higher price for it.

Although this would explain why some good wines are priced so low, it doesn't help with understanding why some wines are priced so high.

Agricultural and food economist Stefano Corsi, and his colleagues at the University of Milan, have been pushing to understand this dynamic. He notes in his literature review that several researchers studying the topic have reached differing conclusions based on their various methodologies, with some affirming price–quality correlation and others disputing it. Using a massive dataset of 266,301 scores from twelve countries, Corsi attempted to understand how wine prices change with wine scores. He and his team pulled the data from *Wine Spectator*, a publication that reviews wines on a one hundred point scale. To make scoring objective they taste blind.[4]

He was testing to see whether an economic theory called the superstar model, developed in the 1980s by Sherwin Rosen, worked in the world of wine. The model states that a small number of stars at the top of the profession make disproportionately more money than the rest. To explain the theory, Corsi points to Lionel Messi and Cristiano Ronaldo in soccer and Beethoven and Taylor Swift in music as examples of this effect.

The results of the study were positive. "It is quite normal to have a high correlation between the the price and the quality. This is something we expect," commented Corsi. But from there the results got more interesting. As he dug deeper into the data, Corsi could not find a correlation between price and quality for wine scores of 89 or below. The data appeared as a random walk. Above 90 points, every point increase was associated with a higher price: "After 95 the price increased very much with each additional point in the score," Corsi explained.[5]

If this data is true for all wines, once above a certain threshold, the more you pay for a wine, the lower the marginal return for wine quality as measured by points. Or perhaps only scores above 90 mean anything. This might help explain some of the disappointment behind splurging for a bottle and not finding it to be substantially better than a much less expensive bottle. And below a certain threshold, the data from this study indicates that using price to determine quality is not helpful. This might mean that the popular advice to buy the second cheapest bottle on a menu is even less helpful than already thought.

* * *

Part of what makes understanding the relationship between price and quality difficult is their mutual interaction. In 2007, researchers from the California Institute of Technology and Stanford University gave graduate students five samples of the same wine, but told participants that they were tasting five different wines worth $5, $10, $35, $45, and $90.[6] As the grad students evaluated the wines the researchers recorded which parts of their brain lit up, using a functional MRI machine. One of the researchers, Antonio Rangel, recalls: "The area of their brain that is thought to encode for the pleasantness of the experience was more active when they drank wine they believed had higher prices. Strictly speaking, that is the only hard finding of the paper ... it is hard to believe that this is not affecting their actual experience somehow, but we don't have hard evidence for that."[7]

Producers familiar with this research could respond by making their wine more expensive without changing any qualitative element of it, which would further confound the relationship between quality and price. If this works, people claim to like the wine not because it tastes better, but because their brains are lighting up with pleasure of a different sort. They might buy more, encouraging the winery to make more. This process is what some think is behind an irrational wine market, where high priced wines do not correlate with more quality but more audacity.

Those arguing that price and wine are not very well correlated have further evidence to point to. Hildegarde Heymann, the esteemed sensory scientist from UC Davis, has a test she calls the price game that she has been playing with her students. She procures five California wines with varying prices, $25, $50, $100, $200, and $400, as well as a counterpoint wine from Bordeaux usually priced in the middle of the pack. She then asks her students to taste them blind and rank them by how much they like them and by price, as well as identifying the odd wine out. Her prize to them for getting the price order correct is a bottle of Château Lafite Rothschild. "Twenty two years and nobody ever got it right," she reports.[8]

It is this sort of anecdotal evidence that suggests that wineries are paying attention to the lessons learned in Rangel and Plassmann's research and pricing their wines optimistically without the added quality. Or perhaps, given the sociological flexibility of what flavours become associated with the arguably ephemeral idea of "premium," they are pricing their wines in the hope to manifest a reality where their taste becomes quality. Either way, it gives fodder to those suggesting that wine prices should not be trusted.

Those defending the idea that wine prices correlate with deliciousness, either in part or in full, have some points to make in response to this idea. It might work for a period of time to price a wine well above its quality level, but eventually people catch on. There are always wines priced highly where reviews don't match up to price, and in the long run, this evidence drags a wine back to reality. Similarly, for wines to get placements in restaurants and quality wine shops, they need to get past the gatekeepers at these locations, who taste the wines before serving them. These professionals, wanting the best for their customers, are used to this dynamic, and are more readily able to reject overpriced wines. So even though it's quite possible to go out of one's way to get a wine overpriced for what it is, it's rarer to find in the real world.

Perhaps the overpriced wine is made by a super-wealthy person who starts a winery more as a lifestyle than a passion, charging $500 per bottle. Behind the scenes, these types of wineries can fail to earn enough money to cover costs, being propped up by the rich person cosplaying as a vintner. They take their shot at glory and quietly fizzle out without fanfare, the unsold inventory being drunk by friends, destroyed, or hidden away in storage. But this is the exception to the rule in most parts of the world, not the norm. So yes, it's possible to create a poorly priced rank of a particular type of wine, but staying within the mainstream wine economy can help avoid this. According to this argument, weirdly priced wines exist, but they eventually self-destruct, and so are exceptions, not the rule.

Still, many new drinkers getting into wine might look at wines such as the $300,000 bottle at the Grill Restaurant in New York, and scratch their heads. That wine is an 1811 Château d'Yquem, a winery owned by the LVMH luxury brand. This is not a new producer set to fizzle out shortly. But equally, it is hard to imagine that the stratospheric price point is set purely based on objective taste quality. This raises the question of what other factors create value in wine.

* * *

In 1991 the artist Damien Hirst took a tiger shark, placed it in a tank of five percent formaldehyde solution, and called it art. Christened *The Physical Impossibility of Death in the Mind of Someone Living*, it sold in 2005 for an estimated 12 million dollars. Eddie Saunders, a Londoner who operated an electrical supplies shop, had preserved a shark in formaldehyde two years earlier and tried to sell it after hearing of Hirst's success, but he couldn't find a buyer.[9] So why did society value Saunders's shark differently?

One part of the answer is fairly clear. Damien Hirst was an exciting artist. Sponsored and promoted by Charles Saatchi, he presented his work in the right context, with the right backers and marketed his work as significant. The question and debate is to what degree the background and perspective of the artist should matter in evaluating the art. One school argues that art should be evaluated based on its beauty and ability to provoke thought rather than who happened to create it. The other school argues that artistic renown and rarity ought to be valued. Once the art confers legitimacy on the artist, the influence of the artist might overrule otherwise objective judgment.

Many in the wine world have attempted the same sales coup as Damien Hirst. In Reggio Emilia, Italy, a man named Tullio Masoni planted a vineyard on a rooftop, hiring artists to make the trellises and barrels, and he sells the resulting wine for $5,000 per bottle in an art gallery. Justifying this stance of wine as art, he told a journalist that he compares the wine to Marcel Duchamp's 1913 bicycle exhibition: "If you see a bicycle wheel in a living room rather than a repair shop, you realize how beautiful it is. My vineyard is like that: it's unexpected; it stimulates the brain; it sparks new thoughts."[10]

Masoni is applying the ideas of conceptual art to wine. Appreciators of *The Physical Impossibility of Death in the Mind of Someone Living* note that part of its power comes from the fact that you're looking at a tiger shark out-of-context. You may not have considered a shark in such close detail before. The parable of Hirst's art shark illustrates the competing school of thoughts of where wine's value comes from – is it more in the liquid itself, or is it the way that a vintner presents the wine, making us focus on and appreciate what we might not have appreciated without the heightened form of presentation?

* * *

Even those who appreciate the value of an artistic approach to wine might push back at the extent of the pricing. In the case of Masoni, is it worth $5,000? Many would argue this is an insane upcharge for a trivial marketing ploy. Those defending the larger idea of Duchampian value could argue that it's not the artistic idea that is bad – the prices merely reflect modern economic disparity.

In 2023, 58 million adults possessed more than a million dollars, while 1.49 billion had less than $10,000.[11] For the millionaire, Masoni's bottle costs half a percent of their wealth, but someone with a net worth of $10,000 could spend all they have on two bottles. Those defending the high prices can say don't blame the wine – blame inequality.

* * *

While some might appreciate the type of psychological, artistic value demonstrated by Masoni, others reject it, while finding value in other aspects of wine. Robert Ulin, a recently retired professor of anthropology, succinctly summarizes the case: "Wine is a cultural construct," he opines. "The stories that people have that tell you about wine I think are part of the pleasure of consuming it."[12] Through this prism, the sensorial joys of wine are so wrapped up in the culture of vine growing, winemaking and wine drinking, that a denial of the psychological effect is an act of unnecessary deprivation. The power of stories to connect us to the rituals and traditions is worth pursuing with every glass.

Anthropology's history with wine is brief, in large part due to the discipline's western biases – the idea that other cultures could and should be studied objectively and that once the mirror was turned back toward the cultures of anthropology's origin, the quest lacked purpose and the necessary distance for critical analysis. A new generation of scholars eventually broke down that barrier, as the harms of a field that only studied the perceived "other" became apparent. Eventually, professional anthropologists began to study wine and to realize the treasure trove of potential research within. Ulin has come to call wine production and consumption "the sweet spot of cultural anthropology."[13]

Anthropology can help us to understand why we might appreciate sensorially similar wine differently. Knowledge of the craft and the cultural miasma of human effort and struggle that goes into a bottle enhances pleasure in a way that the mass-produced, chemically processed liquid in the other glass misses out on. The place, the story, the traditions, and the culture help transport the drinker to a mental place where the wine hums with life and significance. "The more generic, the more removed we are," says Ulin.¹⁴ From this point of view, cultural appreciation transcends the confines of the glass.

There is an accusation against this view, however, that dims the glow of cultural enjoyment: mightn't highly-compensated marketers manipulate language and imagery to take advantage of our desire to believe in wine's authenticity and profundity? If the cultural value is a matrix-like mirage, should we choose to live in it, or follow in Neo's footsteps and search for a sip of lackluster reality? There are really two questions here: to what degree can most wines be called authentic, and if they are not, how should that change our appreciation of them?

Gilles Laferté, a French sociologist, has gained recognition for his work with Olivier Jacquet on how French wines were sold in the 1930s. He argues that during this period, when European wine-buying markets were in a slump, Burgundians chose to export to America, which was just overturning Prohibition. To do this Burgundian elites focused on French peasant folklore and tradition. "So, they sell to the Americans. The French dream as seen by Americans … And so it's this interesting dialogue between the countries. But suddenly, the idea is to completely create something that doesn't exist in the traditions."¹⁵

The non-existent tradition Laferté is referring to is the creation of the Confrérie des Chevaliers du Tastevin which began in 1934 to promote Burgundian wine. He calls this "a folklore of paper for the press, to sell to newspapers, to sell an imaginary … marketing."¹⁶ Tapping into these ideas to promote wines was no accident. The Confrérie knew the power of history, tradition, and cultural rituals in creating value and despite its origins, the Confrérie has grown to have a loyal following and help create a sense of wonder for Burgundian wines.

The question of to what degree institutions are more recent facades and to what degree and at what point they become culturally meaningful is tackled by a number of professors in the book *The Invention of Tradition*, where Eric Hobsbawm observes, "'Traditions' which appear or claim to be old are often quite recent in origin and sometimes invented."[17] So it is clear that the Confrérie is in good company.

In Burgundy, the fact that there is a real and genuine history of vine-growing and winemaking is perhaps what allowed the Confrérie to thrive – it seems legitimate given the context and as time passed it took on more legitimacy. People want to believe in modern demonstrations of cultural history, which encourages those cultural demonstrations to last. What gives these movements power, as Laferté observes, is that "In many domains of cultural, artistic production there is a critique of modernity, and to be primitive is to be modern and being traditional is being modern."[18] So, some people might view the Confrérie and other attempts at cultural enrichment as sales tactics and others might come to appreciate them, even if they have sales as a motive – they add to the richness of wine for these people.

* * *

Marion Demossier, a prolific and eloquent French anthropologist based at the University of Southampton in the United Kingdom, is at home on this topic, and after doing fieldwork in Burgundy, reflects on Laferté's contribution to the research: "His argument is that it was invented by the notable – the local nobility – and the local … elite … After this long process of construction documented from the 1930s [they] basically internalized entirely that folklore and have made that folklore their folklore."[19]

This declaration raises a few psychological and anthropological questions that are pertinent beyond Burgundy and extend to the debate over where wine value comes from. Is the meaningfulness of tradition lessened by possible origins in sales and marketing? Does a tradition's duration affect the power it holds over our imagination? Does the fact that a tradition is created by a local elite rather than as a pure expression of a worker's way of life deprive it of meaning? Or do we acknowledge that the elites were part of the society, too, at the time, so the tradition is meaningful?

People will answer any of these questions in different ways, which in part explains why different people pay different amounts for wine. Those who value the cultural history might pay more, whereas those who regard such cultural allusions as manipulations might not. Many would argue that they are largely immune to cultural appeals to value and imagine themselves to be more interested in objective wine quality. For those people, Demossier extends her argument, demonstrating the many ways that wine functions beyond a mere drink.

> *It's about social relations, but hierarchical classification, so what you drink and with whom will automatically classify you. And then the way you engage with the wine – the way you talk about it, the way you demonstrate your knowledge – will also classify you amongst drinkers. So, there are very distinct processes by which people will be able to move that classification or [switch] from one classification to another ... it's all about exercising power, accessing resources, demonstrating your social capital or your cultural capital.*[20]

This view helps justify the value of wines that carry a historical pedigree of importance. Entry level wines rarely intrude in the social pecking order. The more famous, the more respected, the more storied the bottle, the more it becomes a focus of conversation and a statement more about the identity and social worth of the buyer than about the bottle itself.

This theory aligns with French philosopher Pierre Bourdieu's thinking. In his book *Distinction*, he charts how people use wine to demarcate their social class.[21] Under this view, to buy an everyday bottle is to buy a wine – to buy a special bottle is to buy sophistication, class, and power. And the more a bottle is associated with people of sophistication, class, and power the more there is a self-fulfilling socially upward cycle, further entrenching the power and price of the bottle.

Unsurprisingly, many people push back on this idea, some suggesting that they can think objectively and are not swayed by bottles that carry sociological significance. In exploring to what degree people are able to withstand social pressure, it's helpful to review the psychological literature on the influences over objective taste, and for that Charles Spence is the man to turn to. An experimental psychologist at Somerville College, Oxford, Spence has been a prolific writer on how environment affects taste. His research spans the crunch of potato chips to consulting for a Michelin starred restaurant.

Spence is skeptical of experts' alleged ability to differentiate better wine from worse, arguing that everything beside the wine itself has a great influence: "It's when you add all the bits and pieces together, the price, the lighting, the music, the company, the backstory, the labels on the front, the cork, something [to do] with glass."[22] Acknowledging that taste may play some small role, he returns to the idea that time and again, skilled tasters have been fooled by the effects of anything beyond the wine.

Spence's research lends credence to the argument that wine drinkers, both amateur and professional, are more impressionable when assessing quality than they may care to admit. This further justifies the sociological argument that the real driver of wine quality lies in factors beyond the wine itself. Many successful wineries use psychological means to enhance their products.

* * *

Spence is by no means the only researcher looking into these issues. In a 2022 paper in which researchers in Israel paid 62 people to participate in a study, test subjects were given Diet Coke, a Clif Energy Bar, Greek yogurt, Pabst Blue Ribbon Beer, red wine, tequila, Red Bull, and mineral water. The researchers asked participants to rate how much they liked the products on a scale of one to nine. After the participants dutifully performed this seemingly mundane task, they were given a follow-up question – the question the researchers were really interested in.

The researchers instructed participants: "Please rate how desirable the image of the sort of person who eats/drinks the product is for you. In other words, please indicate your agreement with the following statement: 'I want to be seen as the type of person who eats/drinks the product.'"[23] There were no directions on what that mental image should be – it was completely up to the participants.

If consumers' claims about taste were completely unrelated to social reality, we would expect no correlation between the consumer's admiration for the imagined person and their taste of the item. For example, if you did not want to be like the type of person who you perceived drank wine, but you tasted and claimed to love wine, then this would show that there was no relationship between mental desire and taste.

But when the results came in, the data showed that there was a statistically significant correlation between how much a person liked the item in question and how much they wanted to be like the person associated with the product in their head. How could this be? When the researchers were designing their study, they considered these previous findings: "Satisfying the needs for self-confirmation and identity support should result in enhanced pleasure (i.e., a better taste experience). This is because pleasure in general signals greater goal achievement. Accordingly, consumption of food or drink that supports a consumer's identity is functional and should generate enhanced taste experience."[24]

We view our tongue as an impartial judge, dictating our preferences without social bias, but this study implies that part of the pleasure is due to a mental construct. It's also possible that people are not entirely honest when expressing preference. Certain foods or beverages may not be to their taste, but they claim to like or dislike them for social reasons.

Here we return to the question of to what degree wineries and the wine trade are steering consumer tastes beyond controlling wine quality. How often do they charge more in line with marketing-based cues than the real value of the wine? Psychological researcher Dan Ariely chooses to see it another way. A world-renowned behavioral economist, his book *Predictably Irrational* explores the irrational ways in which humans make decisions throughout their lives and across different fields.

With wine, he argues that the extra context created by wineries is not a trick, but a valuable part of the experience of drinking. "We need to maximize the subjective experience. And we have a moral responsibility to maximize it. I was a winemaker, I'm taking people's money and I need to deliver the best psychological subjective experience that I can."[25] From this perspective, the "other" elements of wine that are unrelated to taste are not evil marketing tricks but are as valuable as the wine itself.

Part of the value of wine then, something that adds to its price and its larger cultural value, is that it is something you can fall in love with, in part because of its quirks and eccentricities – its unique character. Wine doesn't have to be perfect, or the best, to be worth loving. "Your wife is not necessarily more beautiful than other people," Ariely says, drawing a parallel, "Why don't you have pictures of other people?"[26]

Ariely does, however, highlight some of the ways that our judgments of wine, or anything for that matter, can be misled, leaving the door open for some wines to be appraised incorrectly. He points to the anchoring effect, in which people rely too heavily on the first piece of information they receive, and reference point framing, whereby the way the information is presented biases the audience.

In wine's context, these could manifest as an education system that introduces new students to particular wines first over others, presenting them the most historical, classic, or stylistically distinct. This could create value for these types of wines more based on social conditioning than their own inherent taste qualities. Especially in wine, where the classics are highly regarded, value is at least partially instilled by cultural standards rather than by the wines on their own. Consumers growing up in a culture that focuses more on certain wines may learn to appreciate that interpretation of one type of wine over another.

Not only do common cognitive biases alter perceptions of wine, this group argues, but our expectations more generally can change our tastes in powerful ways. In one study, participants received two glasses of the same beer, one of which contained a splash of balsamic vinegar. When not informed about the balsamic vinegar, a majority of the participants preferred the spiked beer, but when they were told in advance about the balsamic vinegar, they claimed to prefer the beer without it. This beer-based study begs the question of what tricks might be played with wine that could confound professed preference and value.

Ultimately, our mental experience shapes what we value in wine more than most would perhaps like to admit. That said, the wine world has developed sophisticated ways to subvert these biases to highlight inherent quality's role in value.

There are wine publications that taste blind, removing biases and publishing scores that reflect quality and that are often surprising. Several prominent blind tastings, the 1976 Paris Wine Tasting being the most fabled, have upset the status quo of prevailing values, with places like California and countries outside of western Europe gaining attention. The very existence of a diverse world of wine made from seemingly countless numbers of regions, for this group, is proof that the wine world is able to recover from its bias and find new wines.

On the other hand, the fact that despite the existence of other wines, their relative lack of respect in the market is proof that the psychological biases are helping established players. That the Liv-Ex 1000, a leading database of collectible wine, is still dominated by Italy and France speaks to the fact that change is slow. The delayed uptick of wines from emerging regions further validates this observation.

Others would argue that Italian or French dominance reflects superior taste or superior or subjective experience, or that wines with long histories hold more value in the marketplace because of their proven track records. To justify spending a hefty amount, a wine buyer needs a strong indication of value. What could possibly be a better signal of quality than a long history of a price holding steady? While other wines might spike in price temporarily, it is easier to validate a high price if that price has remained constant for a long time.

There are several other cultural and economic institutions that, some would argue, serve to keep wine prices even higher. The restaurants or shops wineries sell their wines to, the sommeliers they get to endorse their wines, and any number of other acts of social confirmation reinforce price. Consumers with different levels of trait materialism, the extent to which people value objects and money for their worth and ability to increase happiness, would skew very differently in how much they care about these sorts of class-based reinforcers of quality.

* * *

One of the many people studying the associative power of wine value is Nathalie Spielmann, a professor of marketing at NEOMA business school in Reims, Champagne. She became fascinated with the idea of contagion, whereby people avoid a certain product because it touched something undesirable, even if that undesirable thing has been proven to be harmless, like clean toilet paper. This behavior originates in the evolutionary tendency to avoid eating something that could harm us.

Spielmann notes that there is such a thing as positive contagion as well. When a baseball bat has been owned by Babe Ruth or if a piece of art has previously been displayed in a high-end gallery, these past associations create positive contagion, and the value of the item goes up. This effect is so strong that in one experiment, when a group of putters were given a club that they were told belonged to a professional golfer, they putted more successfully than the group with the same club without the association.[27]

Spielmann's research focused on testing whether cuing consumers with the idea that an edible product is elite changed perceptions, making the group claim to like the product more. She and her co-author used mustard and macarons and controlled for price to ensure that one product being more expensive was not the reason for the increased preference. "Overall, our results suggest that a taste experience is improved when foods embody the characteristics of the social elite," she summarizes.[28]

Part of what makes Spielmann's research compelling is that it attempts to wrestle with the different factors that make us enjoy what we eat. How much do we claim to like things due to intrinsic taste, how much due to price and how much due to social group identification? Based on Antonio Rangel's research showing the power of money over consumers, this has often been assumed as the factor that most biases people's wine appreciation and distorts their judgment. Spielmann is no longer so sure. When considering the power of a high price against the power of group bias in how people evaluate wines, she says, "I think social identification is more important."[29]

Many would no doubt contest the idea that they are more likely to like something because the social elite do or suggest that consumers should strive to not put themselves in positions where they can be easily biased. Surely no one would want to be influenced by factors not related to the product, like social groups, or more trivial influences, like the weight of a bottle. Other wine consumers might choose to lean into these biases when they involve positive aspects – feeling "seen" because the winemaker looks like them, appreciating the values that the winery has, or showcasing cultural tradition. These could be construed as biases, but some might view them as legitimate ways to derive inherent pleasure from wine, or any other product for that matter. And so long as they are enjoying the more laudable non-wine influences, why not lean into deriving pleasure from the small biases too?

* * *

In theory, all these different hypotheses for why wine is valuable and commands the prices it does are not in competition. The question is to what degree each holds power. Some might argue that this question is unanswerable because there is no way to study the kaleidoscope of human motivations with accuracy. Others, upon hearing the underlying reasoning, feel they can do a pretty good job understanding which explanatory levers have more power and which have less.

The question beneath all these competing explanations is which drinking conditions encourage social evaluations of wine and which conditions encourage taste-based evaluations of wine. Patrick Schenk, a sociologist at the University of Zurich, guesses that the fuzziness of tasting as one moves up the quality spectrum has something to do with it. "The finer the differences, the more difficult it gets to taste those differences – a certain terroir, a certain blend or something else – the more important the symbolic aspects become."[30] Where there are no meaningful qualitative differences, sociological explanations for preferences fill the gap.

For those who view the quality differences between different tiers of wines as marginally important, these social explanations for extremely expensive and extremely cheap wines play an outsized role. People who taste wine and believe there are significant, objective differences in quality might argue that the sociological aspects of value are window dressing.

Not only does it matter how people taste and regard objective quality, but also what drinking motivations they bring to the table. Spielmann observes, "With globalization, we had this emerging variety of different consumers. And so we had to amend how we sold wine – how we talked about wine – because a Chinese consumer wasn't drinking or consuming wine for the same reasons, or with the same intentions or with the same pleasure expectations."[31]

This partly explains why there are so many different messages and stories from wineries. They are catering to a different audience, or at very least different audiences at different times. For those not already convinced that their taste is the best, they have an incentive to tell the wine consumer that it is, so that this newfound expectation can fulfill itself when the bottle is opened.

When Karl Storchmann, editor of the *Journal of Wine Economics*, says "quality is what people are willing to pay for wine"[32] it takes both these values into account. The question for wineries is that when it comes to the portion of wine value that is sociologically created, can they create that value and, if so, should they? Many might take the claim that sociological power should come naturally, without an overt marketing attempt by the winery. If a winery lasts a century and is full of stories and traditions, that's great, but making heavy bottles of wine or leaning into elaborate stories goes too far – it feels concocted and not real.

Others, who have studied psychology, seem more open to leaning into the psychological experience just as much as, or perhaps more so than, the taste experience. When musing on the effort and thought that some of his house guests go through to bring a nice bottle for dinner, Charles Spence suggests, "Just put it in a heavy bottle and tell me it's expensive. I'll be perfectly happy."[33] For this school of thought, leaning into the experience, the story, the ceremony, and the rituals around wine is not a needless and greedy marketing push, but an integral part of the creation of value.

Roland Barthes, a French literary critic who studied the role of signs and symbols in society, wrote an essay in his 1957 book, *Mythologies*, where he referred to wine as a totem-drink, representing something distinctive about culture. It is perhaps this philosophical impetus that led Frédéric Brochet (see p. 127), the winemaker who confounded wine tasters' perceptions in his wine-doctoring experiments, to observe, "It's a bit more easy to make people dream with wine than with milk." Because that is the question – when people are paying astronomical prices for wine, when people are cherishing it for years, when people get tattoos of their favorite producer – are they awake, tasting every drop and deriving their experience from the molecular destiny of tannin, acid, and esters, or are they dreaming?

8
Naturalness in wine: on the spectrum of industry and purity

"Science grows and Beauty dwindles"

    Alfred Lord Tennyson, *Locksley Hall – Sixty Years After*

"Yet for better or for worse we do love things that bear the marks of grime, soot, and weather, and we love the colors and the sheen that call to mind the past that made them."

    Jun'ichirō Tanizaki, *In Praise of Shadows*

"Desire for beauty will endure and undermine the desire for truth."

    Richard Prum, *The Evolution of Beauty*

In 1820, Fredrick Accum, a German chemist living in England, published *A Treatise on Adulterations of Food, and Culinary Poisons*. Lambasting a host of adulterated and dangerous products from pickles to pepper, he became an early consumer rights advocate, shining a light on poorly regulated and often unchallenged food and beverage makers. He did not spare wine.

"It is sufficiently obvious, that few of those commodities, which are the objects of commerce, are adulterated to a greater extent than wine," he proclaimed, going on to report a long list of additives known to be used in wines, including lead, gypsum, oak sawdust, and hazelnut husks.[1] Some of the additives were reported to be harmful to the health of the drinker whereas others were simply adjustments intended to improve the wine.

The Mosel region in Germany saw a streak of terrible vintages in the 1840s, exacerbating the already bracing acidity of one of the coolest wine regions of Europe. At this time, some had observed that the higher a wine's acidity, the lower the price.[2] One way some German producers overcame this was by borrowing the French method of sugar addition, adding water to the grape must, as well, so that it would ferment to be more alcoholic, less acidic, and more palatable. Intended to improve the saleability of German wine, this type of adjustment was quickly attacked, with one critic commenting that the Mosel's wines were "the most abominably 'faked' of all real or pretended juices of the grape."[3] As if this wasn't enough criticism, the wines were attacked on a moral level: "We must trust in our all mighty God, who in his great inimitable kitchen of nature, through the powerful effects of the earth and of the alternation of rain with sun, makes wines each year which may not always be equally good, but nevertheless always have their own unique characteristics,"[4] commented one critic, while another stated "We must protect our wines' virginity [Weinkeuschheit] against such copulation."[5]

In the United States, Harvey Washington Wiley would take on the role of consumer advocate. Known for championing the Pure Food and Drug Act of 1906, signed into law by President Theodore Roosevelt, Wiley wrote a set of books calling unscrupulous practitioners to account for their additives. The first book addressed food goods, but the second, published in 1919, was entirely devoted to beverages. In it, he called out the wines of Germany as well as the wines of Jerez, Spain for being adulterated[6] before turning his pen on the American wine scene:

> *In many parts of our country it is a settled conviction among the grape growers that wine cannot be made from the juice of the grape without certain additions, chiefly of sugar ...*

Investigations have shown that it is the custom in some localities to take the pomace, after the expression of the grape must, or of the finished wine, and treat it with additional quantities of sugar and water, allow it to undergo a secondary fermentation, and sell it separately as wine, or mix it with the original product. When, in addition to this, it is considered that not only sugar, but other substances, namely, dextrose, saccharin, artificial coloring matters, tannin, etc., are added, it is easily seen that the wine is hardly any longer even an imitation, but mostly an artificial product.[7]

* * *

Even before the industrial revolution, debates raged about what additives and treatments were best for wine. In Pliny the Elder's *Natural History*, he alludes to the use of pigments to color wine, pitch and resin to flavor wine, and lye-ash, pounded marble, salt, and sulfur to "adjust" the wine. He concludes that "poisons" were added to wines and that they were not "wholesome"[8] – an indication that even in Roman times, wine additives were hotly contested.

A historical pattern begins to emerge: winemakers develop tools, ingredients, and other winemaking aids to improve the wine or to enhance the production process in some way. And then a countermovement pushes back with calls for purity, naturalness, or a return to basics. The particulars of the accusations may change depending on the historical era the dialogue takes place in, but the principles of the debate tend to remain the same: innovation versus traditional craft, quality or efficiency versus authenticity, industry versus purity. In many ways the tension rests on what truth is and what beauty is.

One way to observe what many call the natural wine movement is through a cultural lens, by witnessing it in action at a natural wine fair. One such event, the Cali Natty Wine Fair in Richmond, California, takes place next to a nondescript industrial building a short walk away from the San Francisco Bay. The modern movement is not only about a philosophical disregard for intervention, but a creative playground, a celebration of uncommon winemaking techniques resulting in a cacophony of vibrantly colored and often cloudy wines in a wide spectrum of flavors, from ethereal to microbially-derived stews. It is clear there are cultural as well as ideological differences at play here, at least at the more maximally natural-leaning end of the spectrum.

In terms of philosophical perspective, the modern movement still has many parallels with the type of protestation exemplified by Wiley, Accum, and Pliny. The differences emerge when reviewing the winemaking techniques and additives in question. The level of innovation in wine technology has leapt forward at a dizzying pace, with many criticizing the use of concentrates, industrial tannins, aroma-creating yeasts, and dealcoholizing machines to name a few of the more modern means of intervention.

RAW WINE, Vin Méthode Nature, and VinNatur are three prominent organizations with definitions for naturalness, but there are other organizations with rules, not to mention the countless writers, winemakers, and sommeliers with their own ideas of what defines natural wine. As with all complex debates, the definition of the terms must be approached cautiously, the way a toreador approaches a bull.

Apart from winemaking limitations, there is often a requirement for certain types of farming for natural wine. RAW defines the term as referring only to organic or biodynamic grapes.[9] The Vin Méthode Nature rules, which were recognized in France by INAO in 2020, include a "Charter of Commitment" that requires the grapes to be organic but says nothing about biodynamics.[10] Based in Italy, VinNatur has its own prescription for farming and additional requirements, such as the requirement that at least 90 percent of the grapes must be grown by the vigneron, not purchased from other growers.[11]

The key question to consider when regarding farming is to what degree these viticultural requirements are fair in terms of capturing what is natural. Those in support may point to a chasm between a vineyard farmed with naturally derived applications and laborious weed control and one farmed with a panoply of chemical fungicides, herbicides, and fertilizers. They posit that a natural wine should come from a vineyard that uses only – or at very least mostly – natural farming tools and treatments. Though difficult to draw the line anywhere, some natural advocates say that organics is the best place to do so because it is an objective and legally measurable difference in farming that takes natural values into account.

Those against this idea have a few arguments to turn to. Many organic certifications around the world include exemptions, so there is no guarantee that everything used is natural. It is precisely for this reason that some naturally inclined growers want to go further. They could also argue that organic, or even progressive farming that goes beyond organics, favors machine weeding as opposed to spray, but it may also be fair to say that an advanced piece of machinery isn't a more natural way to control weeds.

As for the marginal cases, for growers that make one organic exception, say, correcting for a severe phosphorus deficiency with an assimilable compound or using one synthetic spray to address an insect infestation, these critics could argue that this is a very reasonable action, and that it in no way limits the naturalness of the resulting grapes. Some might argue that the current zeitgeist has drawn the definitions too narrowly, either because they are misguided or in efforts to limit competition. And as for the limitation placed on purchased fruit, the critic might ask how the transaction of buying grapes invalidates naturalness.

* * *

John Stuart Mill wrestled with this complexity in his essay "On nature," writing:

> It thus appears that we must recognise at least two principal meanings in the word 'nature'. In one sense, it means all the

powers existing in either the outer or the inner world and everything which takes place by means of those powers. In another sense, it means, not everything which happens, but only what takes place without the agency, or without the voluntary and intentional agency, of man.[12]

In this conception, most objects can be said to be natural because of the laws from which they derive, but he identifies humanity as an aberration from nature worth excluding from this conception. In this sense, one could use the first definition to argue that all wine is natural and use the second definition to posit a more limited conception of a natural product.

The Norwegian philosopher Svein Anders Noer Lie, who has written extensively about the philosophical question of naturalness, has identified twelve uses of the word, summarized below:

1. Pristine, as in untampered with by humans;
2. Normal, denoting the way things are;
3. Essence, referencing irreducible being;
4. The opposite of monstrous;
5. Expected, in contrast to the miraculous or supernatural;
6. Unadulterated, as in something's original state;
7. "Historically established," or the way things have turned out;
8. Intrinsic, being characterized by independent, base properties;
9. Unforced, as in what comes most easily;
10. Original, without intention or purpose;
11. Being, rather than mimicking or having been synthesized;
12. The opposite of cultural.[13]

In the context of wine, different groups find different definitions appealing or otherwise depending on what psychological motivation is behind the wine. For Angiolino Maule, an Italian vintner and founder of VinNatur, his inspiration came from reading history. He recalls: "Many years ago, I was struck by a phrase from Louis Pasteur, who in the nineteenth century, wrote that 'wine is the fruit of the land, transformed by human culture.' I realized that wine is essentially solar energy transformed into chemical energy by the stomata in the leaves. From that phrase, I was convinced of the need to make wine just with grapes."[14]

Tracking this motivation over Noer Lie's meanings, natural as an antonym for synthetic jumps out as a chief aspect of meaning for the movement, with an appreciation for history and the human role a part of it. Maule was one of several vintners who, seeing the list of technologies, additives, and adjustments available to wine, marched in the other direction for his naturalistic conception.

As this movement searching for naturalness in wine gained steam, an intellectual problem developed that would need to be overcome. Ann Dumont, the Communications Manager for Lallemand Oenology, which develops microbiological products for the wine industry, summarizes a common refrain by those skeptical of the movement: "the word natural associated with wine is completely inappropriate because if you leave grape juice by itself, then you have vinegar most of the time."[15]

Following this argument, no matter how different the methods employed in the natural wine world, the vines don't prune themselves, the grapes don't pick themselves, and they certainly don't march into vessels and bottle themselves – therefore the entire concept of naturalness is invalid.

We can already see a shifting definition of naturalness – here natural is used to indicate pristine, rather than in the sense that Maule used it. This shifting definitional framework makes the debate tricky because the word natural is co-opted in the way that best serves its user. Depending on the viewpoint of the individual or the winery, different aspects of the word natural are more meaningful or important, so those aspects are accentuated.

There is a critique of the no-wine-is-natural argument, however – the *reductio ad absurdum* argument, attempting to show that the ultimate conclusion of this line of argument ends in ridiculous degrees. If there is no such thing as a natural wine, then a wine picked by hand, fermented with native yeast, and bottled traditionally would be in the same grouping as a wine dyed green, flavored with watermelon extract and processed in a soft drink factory. This critique implies that extremely processed grapes are the same as minimally processed grapes, which very few people would agree with.

* * *

Another argument is sometimes posited: the mirror-opposite of the claim that all wine is unnatural, it argues that all wine is natural. This argument is sometimes used to undermine the position of more niche natural definitions, implying that their definition doesn't matter because if all wine is natural, then no subset of wines can be more natural than the rest.

Starting from the premise that picking, fermenting, and bottling is natural and that the human being is themself a part of nature, one can conclude that the results of that work are natural as well. To use a honey-based analogy, it does not grow on flowers naturally; bees collect nectar, their enzyme, invertase, breaks down the sucrose, the water evaporates, and is stored in honeycomb structures built by the bees. Most people regard honey as natural even if it went through a complex manual and chemical process.

If humans are seen as part of the natural world rather than a force working against it, then the complex and ancient rituals of managing vineyards and turning grapes into wine feel less of an attack on nature and more a part of it. If the tools and ingredients in winemaking are all a result of natural processes and natural laws, then why isn't all wine natural? Bees use enzymes – if humans find and employ enzymes, could they be viewed as natural tools and as such used to create a natural product?

An extension of this argument is to say that anything derived synthetically was still created by humans following laws of nature, so therefore everything is natural. If oak powder and chemically derived acids and tannins are made using the natural laws of physics and chemistry, then anything they are added to must be natural as well. As Svein Anders Noer Lie reflects, "If nature is going by laws all the way down, then everything will also be natural."[16]

This doesn't sit right with many, though. For some, the presence of many wine additives together with the concept of natural seems off, and there is pushback against calling everything natural. This is where attempts have been made to define the contours of what natural wine is, with some groups attempting to define what additives and processes are in and which are out. Regarding naturalness, Svein Anders Noer Lie adds, "It comes in degrees and it is always a compromise."[17]

* * *

Paul Rozin of the University of Pennsylvania has studied what sorts of transformations cause most people to regard the resulting product as unnatural. He submits questionnaires to his subjects, giving them scenarios, and asks them how natural the resulting product is. This is how he found that genetic engineering reduced the reported naturalness of the product by 54.1 percent. He found that respondents reported physical transformations of products (freezing and unfreezing, grinding and juicing) reduced perceived naturalness by about 8.5 percent while chemical changes (adding or removing fat to or from peanut butter, boiling water, and irradiating or pasteurizing milk) diminished the perception of naturalness amongst the respondents by an average of 34.1 percent.[18]

Rozin also investigated different types of mixtures and noted how mixing changed respondents' assessments of the resulting product. The supposed naturalness of bottled water mixed from two sources was diminished by 5.0 percent and making peanut butter using peanuts from two different sources lessened naturalness by 9.5 percent. Rozin contrasted his subjects' attitudes toward mixtures to their attitudes on additions by measuring how the addition of infinitely tiny amounts of unlike substances changed naturalness – calcium added to orange juice and 0.001

percent ocean minerals to water – which produced an average drop in perceived naturalness of 28.2 percent.[19]

Rozin's general conclusions, that the processes involved in making something matter more than its content, as well as the idea that contagion (see p. 151) is a base psychological force in explaining how we decide what sounds natural and what doesn't sound natural, are relevant to the wine conversation. The idea that blending reduces the perception of naturalness might help explain the appeal of place-based wines.

These psychological inclinations appear to help explain some of the natural wine rules to date. For many in the natural wine community, employing fining agents like egg whites or bentonite clay, which clarify the wine, is seen as unnatural. For egg whites, the positive protein in the albumin attracts the negatively charged tannins to form heavier compounds that sink to the bottom of the solution and with clay, the negatively charged particles attract certain proteins that can cause haze, dropping them out of solution. Viewed through Rozin's lens, even though egg white and clay might be natural in origin, they are unlike substances, so many perceive them to reduce the naturalness of the wine.

If naturalness were defined by a vote on what additives feel more natural, then how the question is framed and who is voting matters. For example, if a group were told, "Adding sulfur to wine has been a traditional practice for centuries. It is essential for maintaining a wine's natural character and reflecting the place it comes from. Do you accept this is part of a natural wine?," then likely more people would agree than if they were told sulfur is not strictly necessary and that most commercial types are a by-product of the petroleum industry. The fact that so many people in the natural wine movement can market their wines as natural while adding petroleum by-products is perhaps a hint that the framing element is very important in the definition of how people define naturalness in the first place.

Despite the artifices of framing the issue and controlling the narrative, others still believe that concepts of naturalness can be arrived at in a more objective manner. Patrik Engisch, a philosopher based in Switzerland who is researching the metaphysics of natural wine amongst other topics, responds, arguing, "It's interesting to know what these people's beliefs are but this does not set a precedent for the way we should use the term naturalness."[20] This leaves the intellectual door open for attempts to define natural wine.

* * *

The first question for a winemaker is whether adding yeast is a violation of natural wine rules. Vintners have been unwittingly using the fungus as a winemaking tool for centuries without even knowing it. After Pasteur's discovery that yeast was a mold responsible for fermentation, there was an explosion of further discovery, unleashing an industry that today sells designer specialized yeasts – creating tropical aromas, scavenging iron, and producing lactic acid are a few of the modern yeast innovations.

Some argue that adding yeast is the first step to unnaturalness because it changes the sensorial properties of wine. Alice Feiring, a wine writer and advocate for naturalness in wine, is leery of intervening in this way: "To add extra yeast is really just modifying all the chemistry. You're really determining who's gonna win the race there."[21]

This explanation aligns with Mill's agent theory of naturalness, that something left on its own without human action is more natural than that with an intervention. The unanswered question implicit within Feiring's critique is to what extent adding yeast to wine changes what it would have tasted like anyway if no yeast had been added. Is it possible to taste the difference between an inoculated wine and an uninoculated one, or is the distinction more philosophical?

Ann Dumont, of Lallemand, suggests that using native yeast – the yeast present on the grapes or in the winery – without monitoring the nutrition or nitrogen level of the juice is like the wild west. *Hanseniaspora* yeasts might take over the fermentation, creating unusually high volatile acidity, microorganisms might go after the sugars, creating funky aromas, a struggling fermentation might produce hydrogen sulfide, and so many other microbial calamities could result in an off wine. "You can do everything right in the vineyard, but goodness knows what's gonna happen in the winery."[22]

Another response to the attack on yeast is to suggest that it's much ado about nothing. One researcher studying yeast is Cristian Varela, a Chilean working at the University of Adelaide in Australia. Varela was inspired to study native yeast when looking into a drink made by the aboriginal peoples of Tasmania, where the sap of eucalyptus trees was fermented into a traditional beverage. He wanted to know which native yeasts were fermenting the beverage, and his research led him to a series of research papers investigating how native yeasts operate in wine fermentation.

Varela wonders aloud why yeast has become so maligned in certain circles. "We tend to find this issue with wine, but not with other products, right? Nobody thinks about adding yeast to beer … Bread, that's the other one … all the different types of bread depend on different types of yeasts. So no issues with using yeast for that either."[23] There does not appear to be a movement regarding small bakeries as purveyors of unnatural products, though some devoted sourdough bakers might posit that using yeast is a less natural option. The question then becomes why wine is held to a higher standard of naturalness than beer or bread.

Defenders of indigenous yeast may respond to the double standard by suggesting that while yeast is necessary to make most types of bread and beer, it is not necessary to make Sauvignon Blanc, Garnacha or any other still wine. As for the critique that unmediated fermentations don't end well, there is generally a response that they take fermentations seriously, but given the limited ways to encourage fermentation, vintners differ on how necessary fermentation adjustment is.

RAW WINE carves out an exception for sparkling wines, allowing neutral yeasts to be added.[24] This type of situational flexibility to redefine naturalness not based on the naturalness of the input but based on what is necessary to make the wine implies a wider definition of natural – any additive that is not strictly necessary to make a product is less natural than its strictly necessary counterpart.

Some might critique this position, alleging hypocrisy – the same input is rejected in one circumstance and accepted in another. An alternative theory of naturalness posits that something is natural if all the ingredients that go into it are natural. In the same way that a home-cooked stew is natural, as opposed to ultra-processed, because all the ingredients are themselves natural, someone could argue that a wine is natural so long as its components are natural.

Reflecting on the process of finding, selecting, and breeding wild yeasts for sale to wineries, Ann Dumont comments, "If we're gonna use that word, natural, they're all natural. It's not a chemical, it's not synthetic. They're selected from the vineyards and the wineries. So they are microorganisms that are not modified in one way or another."[25] Using this logic, the definition of natural wine should be expanded to include inoculated wines.

There are a couple of responses to this. The first would be to say that store-bought yeast is not as natural as a yeast occurring in the wild. Even if those yeasts were selected from the wild, they were brought to laboratory-like conditions, propagated, dried, packaged, and sold. This level of processing might be more triggering to some than to others.

One could also suggest that in winemaking, the principle of naturalness is less about the additive, in this case yeast, and more about ideas of human agency. The most natural wine is the one that's had the least human intervention. That said, different nature-inclined advocates insist on more purity, suggesting that pétillant naturel wines, which are bottled with some residual sugar and allowed to ferment in bottle, are the only true natural sparkling wines, Champagne be damned. Disagreement over how much to weigh human intervention and the naturalness of the additive brings the conversation back to the central definitions in question.

A complicating factor is that not all winemakers are honest about using selected yeasts, not because they don't believe in them but because they worry what consumers might think. One source recounts what a winemaker told them in confidence: "I use selected yeast, but for people who come to the cellar and visit, or journalists, it's a lot more romantic if I say that the yeast comes from the vineyard." Many trust winemakers implicitly, but because winemakers are aware of the negative view of additives, they might choose to conceal or not to discuss methods. So, anyone drinking this wine and assuming it is the result of low-intervention winemaking might not have the whole story. And while on an individual level this sort of information withholding might make sense for the winery, collectively this lack of discussion about yeast or lack of pride in discussing it could lead to a perception that most good wineries are not using selected yeasts.

For those who actually do let indigenous yeasts complete their ferments, part of their reasoning is that these yeasts are often regarded as part of the sense of place. Camille Lapierre of Domaine Lapierre in Beaujolais, France, a winery often celebrated and appreciated for its history of natural methods, says, "I love wine with natural yeast because for me this makes wine from the place."[26] The example of designer yeast is often used to prove this point. Some yeasts are selected for their traits of creating particular flavors – for example, making pronounced passionfruit aromas in the context of Sauvignon Blanc. Even if the yeast is natural, the fact that a group of otherwise different wines might develop a sameness based on the result of an additive would be a point that undermines its sense of place.

The counterargument that the yeast-inclined might offer is that not all yeasts have flavor-inducing properties, and according to RAW's dictums about sparkling wine, the selected strain could be a fairly neutral yeast whose mission is just to ferment and not create a particular profile. If the most natural wine is the one that expresses terroir the best, then it could be argued that sometimes adding a yeast might express terroir better if it were to prevent the fermentation from failing or stop another, more deleterious yeast species from taking over. Many argue that if particular yeasts like *Brettanomyces* or *Kloeckera* or some other microbial taint were to take over a fermentation, then that wine would only risk negative outcomes by remaining "natural."

Those who prefer to rely on native yeast and refer to this as a more natural method have a response, though. Sure, there are winemakers who struggle with their fermentations, but barring exceptional circumstances, native yeast works. If the work is done in the vineyard properly, the grape should have everything it needs to ferment, and a good winemaker should be able to stand back and let it happen.

Cristian Varela, a researcher at the University of Adelaide, conjectures about the various likelihoods of failed fermentations: "Even with commercial winemaking, with everything controlled, you still see probably just under 10 percent of stuck ferments for one reason or another – low YAN levels, high potassium, low pH – those sort of combinations tend to affect fermentation kinetics."[27] This is not to say that a vigneron has no power over these determinants of fermentation success. YAN, which stands for yeast assimilable nitrogen, is one of the main factors affecting whether fermentation proceeds smoothly and can be affected by several factors, including keeping vines properly fertilized, but there may be other reasons behind low YAN levels, making unassisted fermentation challenging.

And there are other considerations that help winemakers with native yeast fermentations, such as temperature control and winery cleanliness. Some argue that this should be enough, and that these minimal, circumstantial interventions be allowed in making natural wine. As Alice Feiring states, "You don't need to use nutrients. You already have everything you need. A package of yeast is *always* not a good thing."[28]

There is another school of natural winemaking which prefers to use native yeast but is also willing to adjust the juice prior to fermentation to encourage the native yeast to thrive. One of the most common ways winemakers adjust their YAN levels to avoid faulty fermentations is to add diammonium phosphate, a source of nitrogen, often in combination with vitamins and minerals. Diammonium phosphate is the product of a reaction between ammonia and phosphoric acid. Though this is the most common addition, other proprietary product options are available.

Those who choose to supplement their native ferments argue that this is a small addition with enormous benefit. Not only does it encourage an efficient fermentation by the indigenous yeast found naturally in the juice, but it does so without any problematic aromas linked to a particular yeast or microbial element in the wine. Those in favor of the naturalness of this approach argue that just like temperature control or fertilizing vines, it is a small nudge in the right direction to ensure the natural course of events in fermentation. As the wine writer Andrew Jefford points out, "I can't see any objection to a carefully calibrated YAN addition that helps native yeast perform at its best. I would indeed describe this as a neutral act."[29] Critics of this view would argue that, regardless of type, no additive can be natural, and that by changing the chemical makeup of the juice, the yeasts don't behave as they would have otherwise, so this is an unnatural act.

* * *

The question of the naturalness of yeast in wine is complex because yeast is complex, but there is another additive that has taken up attention in the debate of natural: sulfur dioxide. There is more disagreement over and attention paid to this chemical than perhaps any other aspect of winemaking. Sulfur dioxide has been used in winemaking since the 1600s.[30] It acts both as an antimicrobial agent, killing off microbes that might otherwise scavenge sugar and create a pungent aroma, and as an antioxidant, ensuring that bottled wines don't deteriorate prematurely or turn into vinegar.

Though there are natural sources of sulfur, most commercial sulfur dioxide is made from the sulfur produced as a by-product from petroleum and natural gas processing plants. From there, it is turned into sulfur dioxide and sold to wineries. The fact that a petroleum by-product has been largely accepted by many who care about the naturalness of their wines would seem to further underline the point that conceptions of what's natural don't rely upon the complete naturalness of the additive, but upon using the least possible manipulation to finish a wine – what is commonly called low-intervention winemaking.

Critics of natural wine would point to this as an example of hypocrisy, suggesting that a petroleum by-product used with the intent of killing microbes and limiting a wine's natural evolution cannot possibly be considered natural. This is why one natural wine school of thought has shunned sulfur dioxide, claiming that for a wine to be called natural, it must have nothing added and nothing removed, or what is sometimes called the zero-zero approach.

Part of what animates this movement is the idea that the wine is still alive – the yeast and other microbial life are still active in the wine and are consumed by the drinker. There is, however, a downside to this, which is why so many in the winemaking world have chosen not to pursue this stance: not all microbial life tastes very good. Even those who want to make a natural product and who are open to alternative tastes believe that at some point, wine needs to taste somewhat good. Playing chance with living microbe soup can be like playing Russian roulette with taste – sure, sometimes the result is fine, even good, but at some point a particular aroma really does need to be stopped to please the palates of most human drinkers.

For those winemakers who value naturalness but do not want to risk the possible negative consequences of bottling a wine without a little sulfur dioxide, the question becomes whether the addition of sulfur dioxide is a necessary unnatural act that is the least harmful means to make a good wine, or if the sulfur dioxide can be justified on any other grounds.

Patrik Engisch has been working on the ontological *raison d'être* for natural wine. He says, "Here is a process where only a set of natural properties are unfolding and what you're offering then is an artifact such that when I appreciate it, I'm appreciating nature in the form of natural properties."[31] The resulting question then is whether the winemaker is allowed to pause that chain of natural properties when it has reached a stage that is delicious by adding sulfur dioxide to stop further advancement. In the same way that a photographer captures a deer in the forest, no one is mistaken that the photograph is literally the deer, but the picture is a representation of what the natural world looks like, and that is good enough.

The quantitative aspect of sulfur dioxide is also somewhat unique. There is disagreement amongst vintners and industry professionals over what the threshold of sulfur dioxide should be in natural wine. In France, the Vin Méthode Nature has a logo that wineries may use on labeling without added sulfites, but if sulfites have been added it must be appended to the logo, with a ceiling of 30 milligrams per liter.[32] For VinNatur, above 50 milligrams per liter sulfur dioxide is considered unnatural for whites, rosés, sparkling, and sweet wines, with 30 milligrams per liter and above of sulfur dioxide considered off limits for reds. For RAW, no wine may exceed 50 milligrams of sulfur dioxode per liter.[33] For context, government sulfur dioxide limits are much higher, with Argentina on the low end at 130 milligrams per liter for red wine and the EU on the high end at 400 milligrams per liter for certain sweet wines.[34]

Though those favoring strict limits on sulfur dioxide argue that it impinges on wine's natural expressiveness, there is another view that questions whether the anti-sulfur dioxide school encourages less expressive wines. While researching his book on Austrian wine, Stephen Brook attended a tasting of wines described as natural: "My problem with them was that all the wines taste the same. So they would show me wines from different grape varieties and different vineyards and so on. It made no difference. The oxidative character had completely taken over the wine, and I would find that unacceptable."[35]

This type of argument, shared by more people than Mr. Brook, is a shot across the bow of the most serious kind. In wine, an attack on terroir is the ultimate insult. The retort from those in the natural wine community would be to say that this tasting was an aberration, and that natural wines made well do reflect terroir. While some might acknowledge that a few wines, perhaps many, are not made well, the existence of associations to improve quality and consistency and more conversation about expelling bad producers from their ranks is the modern naturalist's response to Brook's Austrian observation.

* * *

While yeast and sulfur dioxide take up a lot of space in the natural wine conversation, there are other additives that winemakers may debate the inclusion of within the definition of natural. The addition of sugar or acid (usually tartaric acid derived from grapes) is often questioned. Through the twentieth century, winemakers in Germany and France realized that in cool years where the grapes did not fully ripen, adding sugar (chaptalization) was a useful way of ensuring their wines had enough mouthfeel to be pleasurable. On the one hand, if the winemaker's only goal is deliciousness, then there are not many protests against a winemaker chaptalizing to suit her idea of optimal taste. But fine wine often promises more. If a wine's taste and structure are a gustatory stamp of the land, then some might view chemical adjustment not just a change in flavor but a betrayal of terroir. This ideal of showcasing the land through wine is what Angiolino Maule and so many others aspire to.

It is not difficult to see how these additions contradict people's sense of naturalness – they alter wine's structure. But winemakers can defend their use of additives; for decades, amelioration has improved business conditions for struggling grape growers and vintners, enabling them to continue their livelihoods. Or if livelihoods aren't at stake, a winemaker could defend adding sugar or acid by pointing to other elements in wine as the chief determinants of terroir and site, such as aromatic precursors in the grapes themselves. After all, flavor is a primary focus in wine. Depending on how one feels about what constitutes terroir or the winemaker's promise to reflect place, the consumer might accept or reject this argument.

There are a whole host of other winemaking tools and techniques available, but the foundational arguments remain the same. How should a winemaker balance deliciousness and naturalness? Often overlooked are the effects of vessel choice, be it barrel, stainless steel, concrete, or qvevri, and of everyday technological improvements such as electricity, temperature control, and glass, which all change winemaking outcomes. Ancient technologies like the basket press were transformed after the industrial revolution, with inert gases used for freshness throughout most modern wineries. Wineries can use the bacteria *Oenococcus oeni* to start the secondary, malolactic fermentation rather than letting it kick off randomly. Another whole portfolio of products helps increase efficiency at wineries. Anti-foaming agents keep gassy yeast in check and specially tailored enzymes increase juice yields at the press.

Powdered tannins can be purchased and poured into tank to lend more body. Mega Purple, a grape-juice concentrate product, can be used to increase color, boost body, and obscure flaws. Oak powder and oak chips are other ways of introducing oak flavor without extended time in barrel. Apart from changing the structural elements of wine or improving flavor, other products exist to remove any undesirable characteristics that may develop during fermentation or maturation. Copper sulfate can clear up the rotten egg aroma caused by hydrogen sulfide.

When evaluating all these potential additives, the question is whether there can be a unified theory behind why they should or should not be allowed in a natural product. Luca Zanin, who runs a wine additive company, has one possible answer to this question:

> *Malic acid comes from butane, so that's not natural ... It's [from] petroleum-based raw materials and then chemically*

synthesized, so that, to me, doesn't qualify as natural. Tartaric acid does, because we're not making it, we're just refining it. Even the FDA has had a ruling on this. If you're a food company, and you add tartaric acid, you can label it as a natural flavor. If you add malic acid, you have to list it as malic acid.[36]

Some accept this rationale that naturalness ought to be defined by the naturalness of the inputs used, while others consider this overly permissive, preferring to return to the idea that additives shouldn't alter vinous expression. And for others, if a minor synthetic tool is employed like an anti-foaming agent, while it might not be chemically organic, if it's practical without being detectable in the finished wine, its use shouldn't invalidate the wine's natural status. As we've seen, many disagree with this point of view, seeing nothing added, nothing removed as the only real natural standard.

In addition to the additives, wine can be subjected to an array of processes. At minimum, grapes are macerated, pressed, aged, and bottled, but behind this simple framework lies a world of tools: batons for stirring barrels and mixers for stirring tanks, advanced bottling lines, nitrogen, carbon dioxide, and argon gas canisters, and the standard set of cleaning solutions for the cellar.

Many wineries use filters, though there are many different types and levels of filtration. Filters range from broad barriers that remove large particles to 0.45-micron fittings, which stop all yeast and bacteria, virtually sterilizing the wine. Another tool allows the winemaker to infuse tanks or barrels with oxygen. Cryo-extraction is another tool in the arsenal. This involves freezing the grapes so that ice crystals form in the cells of the fruit itself. Once thawed, these cells release additional, otherwise unavailable compounds, from the grape into the macerating juice.

To lower or eliminate alcohol, one can pass wine through a spinning cone, which when done under low temperature and under vacuum, allows volatile compounds like alcohol to be removed from solution. Another technology that accomplishes a similar end is reverse osmosis. Patented in the wine world by Clark Smith, this apparatus forces wine against a very tight membrane at high pressure. Water and alcohol can pass through the membrane but the other chemical components of wine cannot. The water and alcohol can then be separated via evaporation and the water added back to the wine leaving the alcohol behind.

Smith, who founded and sold the company Vinovation, which capitalized on his patent of reverse osmosis, suspects that one reason why certain technologies are accepted in natural wine and others aren't is because of a lack of education and familiarity. In reference to the general wine consumer, he contends, "They had a refrigerator, they had stainless steel, and they had electricity in their kitchen – they had all that stuff – so they're perfectly comfortable with it even though there's nothing traditional about it."[37] Smith is alluding to the fact that most definitions of natural wine do not have restrictions on electricity, stainless steel or even gases like nitrogen or carbon dioxode, which he regards as hypocritical when there are severe restrictions placed on other elements of modernity.

Others would push back against familiarity as an explanation of why some tools are natural and others are not. One of the possible responses is that tanks, electricity, and temperature are acceptable because they don't change wine's nature. For these people, electricity and stainless steel tanks are not that different from a clay or rock vessel and candlelight – it's a convenience, but the chemical composition of the wine isn't changing. But putting wine through a machine to lower alcohol and adding tannin to increase texture are chemical transformations that violate an expectation of what the grape would otherwise give.

Given the powerful effects of many of the winemaking aids reviewed so far, it is no surprise that many oppose excess manipulation, resulting in more of a "Franken-wine" than a reflection of nature. A wine picked so ripe that the grapes are turning to raisins, with added acid, alcohol lowered to 12%, and loaded with oak extract will not smell like the land, these critics argue.

There are generally three responses to this argument: the taste defense, the terroir-is-a-cultural-construct defense, and the it's-not-me-it's-somebody-else defense. The taste defense alleges that the reason the winemaker chose to use those products was because the winemaker knows their wine best and knows that using those additives will make a better product, terroir be damned. The corollary and second argument states that if these additives and techniques become associated with a place, then the cultural use of those products becomes part of the place itself. In the way that Rioja drinkers became used to the impact of American oak, so too they can get used to these other alterations. As time passes, they will be seen less as modern contrivances and more as traditional methods.

The third response is that most fine wine doesn't use these types of tools. Sure, they say, industrial tannins, Mega Purple, and other flavor-adjusting additives are the realm of the mass-produced wine, and these affordable wines tend not to make the terroir argument to begin with. The implication that the world is awash in industrial dreck except for the natural wine producers is a convenient sales point to separate them from the rest of wine and carve out a marketing niche.

This is a difficult claim to adjudicate because historically there has been no ingredient labeling on wine. Even if it comes, this law would likely be difficult to enforce, so producers could get away with a degree of additive use without publicly reporting it. Some within natural wine associations claim that the public should assume that wines outside the associations have additives because otherwise they'd be part of the association. Other wineries can respond in two ways, firstly that while they aren't adding copious amounts of foreign matter to their products, they disagree with the restrictive definitions. Secondly, many producers find most wines in the natural wine community off-putting, and they don't want to associate their products with a community with which they disagree on the basic tenets of what good taste is.

* * *

While the first way to judge natural wine is to question what natural wine should and should not be, the second question is whether these wines are any good. Many defenders of natural wine claim to not only like wilder flavors, but to dislike wines that do not come from the movement. Vincent Wallard is the Co-President of Le Syndicat de Défense des Vins Naturels, which is behind the natural wine logo (Vin Méthode Nature) that appears on qualifying wine bottles in France. He also makes wine in the Loire region of France and says, "I've been transforming my taste from conventional wines to natural wines, little by little. It took me at least ten years to be able to appreciate really natural wines and to cope with all the ups and downs that you've got in those wines. I can say that I'm not able to drink conventional wine anymore."[38] Certainly not everyone preferring more natural wines makes the argument that they are better, but many do, and Wallard's claim is typical of many in the movement.

For critics of these wines, to see natural wine producers claim both that their wines are superior and also that there are higher risks when making wine naturally is like having their cake and eating it too. For many of these critics, natural wine is not only bad, but terrible.

Valerie Joly of Coulée de Serrant, who makes wines she believes are natural, is skeptical of the way natural has been defined and of wines that have come out of the movement: "It's pretty rare that I really do enjoy a natural wine. There are very few very good producers that manage to have a very good natural wine with aging capacity and things like that. There are so many wines that – they just don't care about it and they bottle it and it's a mix of everything and very trendy. It works very well in some trendy bars in Paris."[39]

There is a belief that many and perhaps most in France who label this way are using natural as a niche marketing gimmick to be able to sell their wines and avoid French winemaking rules. The reference to trendy wine bars in Paris is not positive. Given the psychological power behind where and how a wine is served, there is an argument that though most natural wine is terrible, if it's presented as stylish, some drinkers may disregard their senses and claim to enjoy it. If the wines were served in a blind tasting, says this view, the outcome would likely be different.

Apologists for naturally inflected wines have defended them, suggesting that people should be open to new flavors. As Wallard says, "The very strange thing with natural wine is that there's always a consumer for each wine. Even if for you it looks very bad, there will be somebody who will find it interesting, nice or to his taste."[40] From this perspective, taste profiles that in the past have been regarded as universally bad should be viewed more subjectively. Perhaps these wines don't appeal to everyone, but if there are a few people who don't mind the flavors, then there is nothing wrong.

Critics argue that this apologist tone misses the point that the movement has allowed objective flaws into the marketplace. Mousiness, volatile acidity, and other faults have been commonly noted in wine marketed as natural, and the critic would argue they are objectively bad, especially when tasted blind. As the sensory scientist Hildegarde Heymann notes, "If a wine is flawed, it can never be a quality wine."[41] Even if by chance there are a few good examples, the critique is that in general, the movement has championed flawed wine unabashedly. Just as some critics of art or architecture point to periods of weakness throughout history, some wine critics mark the movement's dominance in this era as a dark age for wine that needs to be overcome.

Some in the movement acknowledge that there are bad natural wines and are working to change what is allowed under the banner of natural wine. For these people, natural wine should be those wines that taste good, and anything that does not should be disposed of, distilled into liquor, or used in some other way. Still others argue that the movement has already effectively moderated the extremists, and we shall see how quality control will continue to evolve.

* * *

Given the complexity of evaluating the boundaries of good taste and the contours of what is natural, it is helpful to step back for a broader picture. Alan Levinovitz, a professor of religion at James Madison University, has studied the ways that appeals to naturalness are similar to appeals to a god. Looking at the ubiquity of naturalness in advertising – natural cleaners, natural medicines, natural foods, and so on – he contends that just because something is natural does not make it better, and in fact sometimes it can be dangerous. But he finds the religious lens to be a helpful perspective in better understanding nature-inclined movements:

> *I believe that the people who are going to seek out natural wines are going to be people for whom their biggest disenchantment with the world has to do with industrialization and centralization. So, it's going to be people who feel disempowered by technology. It's going to be people who are concerned about the environment and see problems with the environment as a direct result of technology and industrialization ... and seeking out natural wine ... I think of it as a kind of ritual practice meant to ward off what they see as threats to the world.*[42]

In this sense, for those that don't understand the fervor of some people who are excited about "natural" wine, it is because consuming a glass signifies a connection with nature, and by analogy, to a god-like force. Though the movement makes claims of quality, health, and terroir expression, the baser meaning lies within the axiomatic allure of the natural world.

Levinovitz goes on, discussing the biodynamic farming method favored by many in the natural wine movement, analogizing a biodynamic farmer to a shaman. "Shamans are good at what they do and what they're good at is manipulating symbols and narratives to create significance."[43] This level of meaning certainly isn't relevant to the casual wine drinker popping into a natural wine bar for the vibes or because they like the wines, but for those closer to the movement, the winemakers and viticulturists are less tastemakers and more philosophical leaders. This isn't necessarily a normative claim about the goodness or the badness of naturalness, just indicates that its appeal can be reminiscent of the sacred.

One then wonders if the concept of naturalness attracts a certain type of person more than others. "I think the disjunction between political and religious conservatism and naturalness was an anomaly," says Levinovitz, "and it had to do with the association of environmental conservation with political liberalism. I think that's going to shift and has already shifted."[44]

The hypothesis that naturalness appeals more to a conservative mindset is a claim that would no doubt be contested by others. Regardless, the idea that different people seem to have different predilections for naturally derived products further adds to the complexity of natural wine because not only are the definitions contested, but the extent to which society cares about naturalness changes what is in the glass.

Brian Meier, who holds a doctorate in psychology and is a professor at Gettysburg College in Pennsylvania, studies what draws people to natural medicines and products. From stickers and chocolate to performance drinks and injectable drugs, Meier and fellow researchers found a robust preference for natural products across the board.[45]

The reasoning employed by many when explaining their preference is for potential safety – in the case of wine, this would involve safety from undesirable farming or winemaking inputs – but the widespread preference for naturalness seems to go beyond this. In studies where scientists have told participants that the synthetic and natural options have the same level of safety, participants still prefer the natural solution, according to Meier. He has struggled to understand why there is such a strong pull towards naturalness even in conditions where people know there are no additional benefits. "I think it's like morality," Meier reflects. "People have a hard time explaining it."[46]

The other way to think about how the pull of naturalness works is to analyze demographic preferences to see which groups prefer natural products. Meier reflects on all his attempts to find the answer: "We've looked at so many different personality traits. Neuroticism doesn't seem to predict it. All the other personality traits like extroversion or openness or conscientiousness, like responsibility – they don't predict it. Education doesn't predict it ..." The quest to identify which types of people find naturalness compelling is in its infancy. Meier was even involved with a non-peer-reviewed paper that tested whether people with more scientific knowledge were less likely to prefer natural solutions, but they seemed to prefer naturalness just as much.

Given the widespread desire for natural products and the length of time humans have debated naturalness in wine, the conversation is unlikely to go away. Depending on the technologies and innovations in wine, the rules of transparency or lack thereof, and the state of the wine world, the additives and processes in question will change, but the fundamental questions and movements will remain. How should the different definitions of natural be reconciled to decide what a natural wine is? What can human beings and their inventions do to something before it ceases to be a reflection of the natural world? Can nature be captured in a bottle?

A mental digestif

For those who have made it through this book, perhaps some of you have noticed some themes. For those who haven't, I think they are important enough to write out explicitly.

Firstly, irony. For those picking up a book with words like "controversies" and "debates" within its title and worrying about an acerbic, black and white view, I hope you've found it satisfyingly lacking in rancor. The people whom I interviewed were extraordinarily kind and open in sharing their perspectives. They may have astoundingly different lenses through which to view the topic of wine, but they deserve nothing but respect, even if you disagree with them. I hope it became clear that any pretense of a two-sided presentation must be pushed further.

In humanizing all angles of the story, I hope that I framed each issue as originating from a place of good intention, even if colored by human fallibility. In my conversations with many, it became clear that at least part of their fervor was derived from not having taken the time to meet and intellectually question a person who held a disliked belief. Those conversations by no means have to lead to changing one's views – in many cases they should not – but at least they lead to better understanding of human values.

Secondly, in further considering what makes these topics difficult, it becomes clear that every issue, as it opens up like an unfurling octopus, eventually touches upon a base values-oriented question. Even if most issues broached are scientifically resolvable, usually there is at least one strand of argument that touches on a deeper question of how to live, how much risk to take, where we owe our allegiances, or some other human difficulty. Even if most of the issue proves to be fallacious, it is usually that one baser human question that animates the life of the entire concept.

A third theme is intellectual disconnect and silence. Complex ideas aren't often raised in general conversation or marketing language, not because they aren't important but because there's no incentive to publicize the messiness. With regional wine rules and terroir, as long as there's an idealized narrative to aggrandize winery reputations, these same wineries won't choose to publicly critique the system their livelihoods depend on. A perfectly good academic debate stays on the sidelines because there's no reason to have it. For wine quality and value, the moment a winery achieves this feat, there's less of an incentive to question the paradigm of what quality is. It's easier to take the money. In the case of farming, at least in recent history, organic and biodynamic voices are coming to dominate the discourse, but wineries choosing not to adopt those practices don't often engage in open debate in defense of their stance, choosing to pursue less contrary marketing lines. The fact that voices are seldom raised publicly doesn't mean that consensus has been reached. Yet the conversation is still very much worth having.

Finally, perhaps the most important theme is a questioning of how much knowledge to seek before assuming we know the truth in a world filled with so much distorted information. It's hard enough to follow any seemingly standard argument down the labyrinthine rabbit hole, through all its twists and turns, but it is even harder when that path is encrusted with logical and psychological booby traps of misinformation. Wineries are incentivized to boast about the dubious ways their wines are special. Beverage professionals are incentivized to demonstrate their knowledge which often means they're pressured to opine rather than admit ignorance. Wine writers are incentivized to be palatable and entertaining rather than to investigate subjective claims. And mediating all this are the layers of history which become encrusted with myths, half-truths, and conjecture.

At this same time as we acknowledge that the issues touch on hard subjects, it's impossible not to acknowledge that in getting so sucked into the arcana of wine and imbuing it with such meaning, we are often led astray and fall for silly ideas. Perhaps more than most industries or crafts, the wine trade has nurtured and released for the world a steady and consistent supply of shibboleths, helping to foster a community of wine aficionados and sommeliers that cling to accepted truths with the fervor of koalas clinging to eucalyptus trees.

More often than is ideal, the barometer of truth in wine is not multiple peer reviewed studies, but singular charisma, a beguiling figure indefatigably insisting that they know something others don't. Just because a concept invokes large, philosophical life questions doesn't mean that scientists, vintners, and students of wine should be afraid to question its substance and move on.

There is a reason wine library shelves have grown heavy with titles promising to bust myths, spill secrets, and bear the truth – it's because in a sense all these titles have hit on a key issue with wine, that moving towards deeper knowledge is surprisingly hard. If this book can play even a small role in helping its readers move towards a better understanding of wine and of life, and encourage more curiosity to question what we know, holding our urge to jump to an opinion and asking questions first, then it will have been worth it. And perhaps, failing this admittedly lofty objective, it can fulfill a lower and easier hurdle to overcome – perhaps it can convince you to open a bottle of wine.

Notes

Chapter 1

1. Demossier, M. (2012) "The Europeanization of terroir: Consuming place, tradition and authenticity," in *European Identity and Culture*. Routledge, p. 1
2. Brillat-Savarin, as cited in Trubek, A. (2008), *The Taste of Place: A Cultural Journey into Terroir*. University of California Press, p. 19
3. Parker, T. (2015) *Tasting French Terroir: The History of an Idea*. Berkeley, CA: University of California Press (California Studies in Food and Culture, 54), p. 2
4. Landrieu-Lussigny, M.-H., and Pitiot, S. (2014) *The Climats and Lieux-dits of the Great Vineyards of Burgundy*. Éditions du Meurger
5. Chapuis, C., cited in Ballantyne, D., Terblanche, N. S., Lecat, B., and Chapuis, C. (2019) "Old world and new world wine concepts of terroir and wine: perspectives of three renowned non-French wine makers," *Journal of Wine Research*, 30(2), pp. 124–125. Available at: https://www.tandfonline.com/doi/abs/10.1080/09571264.2019.1602031 (Accessed: January 17, 2025)
6. Jacquet, O. (February 25, 2025), interview with A. Ramey
7. Tanabe, C. K., Nelson, J., Boulton, R. B., Ebeler, S. E., and Hopfer, H. (2020) "The use of macro, micro, and trace elemental profiles to differentiate commercial single vineyard Pinot Noir wines at a sub-regional level," *Molecules*, 25(11), p. 2552. Available at: https://doi.org/10.3390/molecules25112552
8. Maltman, A. (January 16, 2025), interview with A. Ramey
9. ibid.
10. Vannier, F. (January 13, 2025), interview with A. Ramey
11. van Leeuwen, C. (1989), cited in van Leeuwen, C. and Seguin, G. (2006) "The concept of terroir in viticulture,"

Journal of Wine Research, 17(1), p. 6. Available at: https://doi.org/10.1080/09571260600633135
12. Winkler, A. J., Cook, J. A., Kliewer, W. M., and Lider, L. A. (1974) *General Viticulture* (2nd edn). University of California Press, p. 74
13. Vannier, interview
14. Tian, T., Ruppel, M., Osborne, J., Tomasino, E., and Schreiner, R. P. (2022) "Fertilize or supplement: The impact of nitrogen on vine productivity and wine sensory properties in Chardonnay," *American Journal of Enology and Viticulture*, 73(3), pp. 156–169. Available at: https://doi.org/10.5344/ajev.2022.21044
15. van Leeuwen and Seguin, p. 7
16. Jones, G. (January 8, 2025), interview with A. Ramey
17. van Leeuwen and Seguin, p. 4
18. van Leeuwen, C., Barbe, J.-C., Darriet, P., et al. (2022) "Aromatic maturity is a cornerstone of terroir expression in red wine." Published in cooperation with Terclim 2022 (XIVth International Terroir Congress and 2nd ClimWine Symposium), 3–8 July 2022, Bordeaux, France. *OENO One*, 56(2), pp. 335–351. Available at: https://doi.org/10.20870/oeno-one.2022.56.2.5441
19. Spielmann, N. and Gelinas-Chebat, C. (2012) "Terroir? That's not how I would describe it," *International Journal of Wine Business Research*, 24, p. 257. Available at: https://doi.org/10.1108/17511061211280310
20. Harding, J. and Robinson, J. (eds) (2023) *The Oxford Companion to Wine (5th edn)*. Oxford: Oxford University Press, p. 752
21. Roberts, D. (January 5, 2024), interview with A. Ramey
22. ibid.
23. Morris, J. (January 22, 2025), interview with A. Ramey
24. ibid.
25. Dalton, L. (2012–present) "Episode 357: Daniel Brunier," *I'll Drink to That! Wine Talk* [Audio Podcast] Anticipation Audio Co., 11:35. Available at: https://illdrinktothatpod.com/episode/357-daniel-brunier (Accessed: January 30, 2025)
26. Jones, interview
27. Deloire, A., Vaudour, E., Carey, V. A., Bonnardot, V., and van Leeuwen, C. (2005) "Grapevine responses to terroir: a global approach," *OENO One*, 39(4), p. 158. Available at: https://doi.org/10.20870/oeno-one.2005.39.4.888

28. Roberts, D. (October 14, 2023), interview with A. Ramey
29. Whalen, P. (2007) "'A merciless source of happy memories': Gaston Roupnel and the folklore of Burgundian terroir." *Journal of Folklore Research*, 44(1), p. 25
30. Demossier, M. in Friedman, R. and Thiel, M. (2013) *European Identity and Culture: Narratives of Transnational Belonging.* Ashgate Publishing, Ltd. p. 123
31. Bois, B. (January 24, 2025), interview with A. Ramey
32. Riviezzo, A., Garofano, A., Granata, J., and Kakavand, S. (2017) "Using terroir to exploit local identity and cultural heritage in marketing strategies: An exploratory study among Italian and French wine producers," *Place Branding and Public Diplomacy*, 13, p. 4. Available at: https://doi.org/10.1057/s41254-016-0036-4
33. Laudan, R. (2004) "Slow food: The French terroir strategy, and culinary modernism," *Food, Culture and Society*, 7(2), p. 138
34. Demossier, M. (2011) "Beyond terroir: territorial construction, hegemonic discourses, and French wine culture," *Journal of the Royal Anthropological Institute*, 17(4), p. 691. Available at: https://doi.org/10.1111/j.1467-9655.2011.01714.x
35. Demossier (2011), p. 701
36. Demossier, M. (June 4, 2025), interview with A. Ramey
37. Jacquet, interview
38. Tanabe et al., p. 3
39. Trubek, interview
40. Crossland-Marr, L. and Krause, E. L. (2023) "Theorizing authenticity: Introduction to the special section," *Gastronomica*, 23(1), p. 8. Available at: https://doi.org/10.1525/gfc.2023.23.1.5
41. Trubek, interview

Chapter 2

1. de Laforcade, A. (July 15, 2024), interview with A. Ramey
2. Saint-Émilion wine classification, Les Vins de Saint-Émilion. https://vins-saint-emilion.com/en/welcome-in-the-vineyard/saint-emilion-wine-classification/ (Accessed: September 30, 2025)
3. de Laforcade, interview
4. Fandl, K. J. (2018) "Regulatory policy and innovation in the wine industry: A comparative analysis of Old and New World wine

regulations," *American University International Law Review*, 34(2), p. 280
5. ibid., p. 304
6. Jacquet, O. (February 25, 2025), interview with A. Ramey
7. Fandl, p. 319
8. ibid., p. 315
9. O'Connor, B. (2004) *The Law of Geographical Indications*. Cameron May, pp. 27–28
10. ibid., p. 31
11. Mendelson, R. (2009) *From Demon to Darling: A Legal History of Wine in America*. University of California Press, p. 141
12. ibid., pp. 147–148
13. McGourty, G. (April 19, 2024), interview with A. Ramey
14. Unwin, T. (1991) *Wine and the Vine: An Historical Geography of Viticulture and the Wine Trade*. Routledge, p. 274
15. Demossier, M. (2011) "Beyond terroir: Territorial construction, hegemonic discourses, and French wine culture," *Journal of the Royal Anthropological Institute*, 17(4), p. 690. Available at: https://doi.org/10.1111/j.1467-9655.2011.01714.x
16. Carter, E. A. (2012) *Cooperation, Competition, and Regulation: Constructing Value in French and Italian Wine Markets*. UC Berkeley (PhD dissertation), p. 39. Available at: https://escholarship.org/uc/item/8w505189 (Accessed: February 2, 2025)
17. ibid., p. 39
18. Zappalaglio, A. (March 5, 2025), interview with A. Ramey
19. ibid.
20. Anderson, K. (February 26, 2025), interview with A. Ramey
21. Zappalaglio, interview
22. Addor, F. (March 13, 2025), email to A. Ramey
23. Enfield, L. (November 11, 2021) "The UK village that lost its cheese," BBC website. Available at: https://www.bbc.com/travel/article/20211110-the-uk-village-that-lost-its-cheese (Accessed: October 1, 2025)
24. Josling, T. (2006) "The war on terroir: Geographical indications as a transatlantic trade conflict," *Journal of Agricultural Economics*, 57(3), p. 338. Available at: https://doi.org/10.1111/j.1477-9552.2006.00075.x
25. Zappalaglio, interview

26. Fandl, p. 285
27. Broude, T. (2005) "Taking 'trade and culture' seriously: Geographical indications and cultural protection in WTO law," *University of Pennsylvania Journal of International Law*, 26(4), p. 623
28. Mendelson, R. (March 12, 2025), interview with A. Ramey
29. Broude, p. 681
30. Torres, C., Arcos, M., Javier, F., and Jégouzo, L. (eds) (2021) *Wine Law*. ESHTE-Estoril Higher Institute for Tourism and Hostel Studies, pp. 69–70. Available at: https://dialnet.unirioja.es/servlet/libro?codigo=874281 (Accessed: February 18, 2025)
31. O'Connor, B. (March 10, 2025), interview with A. Ramey
32. Zappalaglio, interview
33. Broude, p. 692
34. Clarke, J. (2020) *The wines of South Africa*. Académie du Vin Library, pp. 39–41
35. Fandl, p. 282
36. Carter, E. (February 27, 2025), interview with A. Ramey
37. ibid.
38. Anderson, K. (February 27, 2025), interview with A. Ramey
39. Clarke, p. 42
40. Loubère, L. A. (1990) *The Wine Revolution in France: The Twentieth Century*. Princeton University Press, p. 116
41. Josling, p. 339
42. ibid., p. 342

Chapter 3

1. James, W. (1940, 2003) *Look to the Land* (2nd edn). Sophia Perennis, p. 113
2. Hager, T. (2009) *The Alchemy of Air* [Audiobook]. Audible Studios, 6:51:32 (Accessed: September 1, 2025)
3. Haber, F. (1920) "The synthesis of ammonia from its elements." Nobel Lecture, 2 June. Available at: https://www.nobelprize.org/uploads/2018/06/haber-lecture.pdf
4. Lodeman, E. G. (1896, 2023) *The Spraying of Plants: A succinct account of the history, principles and practice of the application of liquids and powders to plants, for the purpose of destroying insects and fungi*. Legare Street Press, pp. ix–x

5. Lodeman, pp. 22–23
6. Jas, N. (2007) "Public health and pesticide regulation in France before and after Silent Spring," *History and Technology*, 23(4), p. 372
7. Lodeman, p. 54
8. Howard, L. E. (1954) *Sir Albert Howard in India*. Plymouth: Latimer Trend & Company Ltd, ch 1, paragraph 3. Available at: https://journeytoforever.org/farm_library/HI/HI2.html (Accessed: August 5, 2024)
9. Barton, G. A. (2018) *The Global History of Organic Farming*. Oxford, New York: Oxford University Press, p. 77
10. ibid., p. 65
11. Howard, A. (1940, 2018) *An Agricultural Testament*. Naples, Italy: Albatross Publishers, p. 182
12. ibid, p. 38
13. Howard, A., pp. 159–160
14. Lockeretz, W. (ed.) (2007) *Organic Farming: An International History*. CAB International, pp. 15–17
15. Fernandez-Cornejo, J., Osteen, C., Wechsler, S. J., et al. (2014) *Pesticide Use in U.S. Agriculture: 21 Selected Crops, 1960–2008*. USDA Economic Research Service, p. 3. Available at: https://www.ers.usda.gov/publications/pub-details?pubid=43855 (Accessed: August 27, 2025)
16. Stafford, E. M. and Jensen, F. (1953) "DDT resistant leafhoppers malathon outstanding for grape leafhopper control in tests in areas where DDT resistance was present," *California Agriculture* 7(4), p. 5
17. Chiba, M. and Doornbos, F. (1971) "Studies on the degradation of DDT during fermentation of grapes and its solubility in wine," *American Journal of Enology and Viticulture*, 22(4), pp. 189–193. Available at: https://doi.org/10.5344/ajev.1971.22.4.189
18. Clark, M. and Tilman, D. (2017) "Comparative analysis of environmental impacts of agricultural production systems, agricultural input efficiency, and food choice," *Environmental Research Letters*, 12(6), p. 1. Available at: https://doi.org/10.1088/1748-9326/aa6cd5
19. Brown, E. C. (2025) *The wines of California*. Académie du Vin Library, p. 119
20. McGourty, G. (ed.) (2011) *Organic Winegrowing Manual*. University of California, Agriculture and Natural Resources, p. 3

21. Guthman, J. (1998) "Regulating meaning, appropriating nature: The codification of California organic agriculture," *Antipode*, 30, p. 141. Available at: https://doi.org/10.1111/1467-8330.00071
22. Lockeretz, p. 155
23. Seufert, V., Ramankutty, N., and Mayerhofer, T. (2017) "What is this thing called organic? – How organic farming is codified in regulations," *Food Policy*, 68, p. 22. Available at: https://doi.org/10.1016/j.foodpol.2016.12.009
24. National Archives Code of Federal Regulations (2000), 7 CFR Part 205 Subpart G – The National List of Allowed and Prohibited Substances. Available at: https://www.ecfr.gov/current/title-7/part-205/subject-group-ECFR0ebc5d139b750cd (Accessed: November 6, 2025)
25. USDA Agricultural Marketing Service (no date) *The National List of Allowed and Prohibited Substances*. Available at: https://www.ams.usda.gov/rules-regulations/national-list-allowed-and-prohibited-substances (Accessed: September 1, 2025)
26. USDA Agricultural Marketing Service (2018) "National Organic Standards Board Crops Subcommittee Petitioned Material Proposal Polyoxin D Zinc Salt." Available at: https://www.ams.usda.gov/sites/default/files/media/CSPolyoxinDZincSaltApril2018.pdf
27. Andrews, N. and Baker, B. (2009) *Can I Use this Product for Disease Management on my Organic Farm?* eOrganic, the Organic Agriculture Community of the Extension Foundation. Available at: https://eorganic.org/node/2472 (Accessed: August 9, 2023)
28. Li, Y., Ye, F., Wang, A., et al. (2016) "Chronic arsenic poisoning probably caused by arsenic-based pesticides: Findings from an investigation study of a household," *International Journal of Environmental Research and Public Health*, 13(1), p. 133. Available at: https://doi.org/10.3390/ijerph13010133
29. Comuzzo, P., Rauhut, D., Werner, M., Lagazio, C., and Zironi, R. (2013) "A survey on wines from organic viticulture from different European countries," *Food Control*, 34(2), p. 274. Available at: https://doi.org/10.1016/j.foodcont.2013.04.039
30. Brinkley, J. (May 9, 2024), interview with A. Ramey
31. ibid.
32. Dixon, L. (April 30, 2024), interview with A. Ramey

33. Seufert et al., p. 14
34. Rice, S. (May 9, 2024), interview with A. Ramey
35. ibid.
36. Seufert, et al., p. 15
37. Padel, et al. (2009), as cited in Seufert, et al., p. 15
38. Jackson, R. (April 27, 2024), interview with A. Ramey
39. ibid.
40. Coll, P., Le Cadre, E., Blanchart, E., Hinsinger, P., and Villenave, C. (2011) "Organic viticulture and soil quality: A long-term study in southern France," *Applied Soil Ecology*, 50, p. 42. Available at: https://www.sciencedirect.com/science/article/abs/pii/S0929139311001570 (Accessed: January 29, 2024)
41. Spinthiropoulou, H. (May 29, 2024), email to A. Ramey
42. Fenton, M., Albers, C., and Ketterings, Q. (2008) "Cornell University Cooperative Extension Agronomy Fact Sheet 41: Soil Organic Matter." Available at: https://franklin.cce.cornell.edu/resources/soil-organic-matter-fact-sheet (Accessed: November 8, 2024)
43. Reganold, J. (August 24, 2024), interview with A. Ramey
44. Fenton, et al.
45. Tuomisto, H. L., Hodge, I. D., Riordan, P., and Macdonald, D. W. (2012) "Does organic farming reduce environmental impacts? – A meta-analysis of European research," *Journal of Environmental Management*, 112, p. 312. Available at: https://doi.org/10.1016/j.jenvman.2012.08.018
46. Trappe, J. (2005) "A.B. Frank and mycorrhizae: The challenge to evolutionary and ecologic theory," *Mycorrhiza*, 15, p. 277. Available at: https://doi.org/10.1007/s00572-004-0330-5
47. Lockeretz, p. 6
48. Döring, J., Collins, C., Frisch, M., and Kauer, R. (2019) "Organic and biodynamic viticulture affect biodiversity and properties of vine and wine: A systematic quantitative review," *American Journal of Enology and Viticulture*, 70, p. 228. Available at: https://doi.org/10.5344/ajev.2019.18047
49. Goldammer, T. (2018) *Grape Grower's Handbook: A Guide to Viticulture for Wine Production* (3rd edn). Apex Publishers, p. 195
50. Hale, L. (October 22, 2024), interview with A. Ramey

51. Wine Australia (2023) "The latest insights for organic wine," *Market Bulletin*, 295. Available at: https://www.wineaustralia.com/news/market-bulletin/issue-295 (Accessed: August 24, 2025)
52. Paarlberg, R. (September 9, 2024), interview with A. Ramey
53. ibid.
54. Goldammer, p. 200
55. Wipulasena, A. and Mashal, M. (December 7, 2021) "Sri Lanka's plunge into organic farming brings disaster," *The New York Times*. Available at: https://www.nytimes.com/2021/12/07/world/asia/sri-lanka-organic-farming-fertilizer.html (Accessed: August 27, 2025)
56. USDA Foreign Agricultural Service (April 8, 2021) "EU Commission Unveils EU Organic Action Plan". Available at: https://apps.fas.usda.gov/newgainapi/api/Report/DownloadReportByFileName?fileName=EU%20Commission%20Unveils%20EU%20Organic%20Action%20Plan%20_Brussels%20USEU_European%20Union_04-03-2021
57. State of California (2022) "California Global Warming Solutions Act of 2006: climate goal: natural and working lands," California Assembly Bill 1757, chapter 341. Available at: https://legiscan.com/CA/text/AB1757/id/2606951#:~:text=The%20act%20requires%20the%20state,later%20than%20December%2031%2C%202030
58. Goldammer, p. 229
59. ibid.
60. Lockeretz, pp. 55–56
61. Coll, et al., p. 37
62. Beaumelle, L., Giffard B., Tolle P., et al. (2023) "Biodiversity conservation, ecosystem services and organic viticulture: A glass half-full," *Agriculture, Ecosystems & Environment*, 351, p. 8. Available at: https://doi.org/10.1016/j.agee.2023.108474
63. Coll, et al., p. 37
64. Clark and Tilman, p. 1
65. U.S. National Ocean Service (NOAA) (no date) "What is eutrophication?". https://oceanservice.noaa.gov/facts/eutrophication.html (Accessed: August 12, 2024)
66. Legeron, I. (2017) *Natural Wine: An introduction to organic and biodynamic wines made naturally* (2nd edn). CICO, p. 9.
67. Lockeretz, p. 57

68. Jackson, R. S. (2020) *Wine Science: Principles and applications* (5th edn). Academic Press, p. 228
69. ibid, p. 230
70. Seufert, et al., p. 17
71. Howard, A., pp. 37–38
72. Lockeretz, pp. 18–19
73. Morrison, K. (May 7, 2024), interview with A. Ramey
74. *New York Times* (26 December, 1913) "Vineyards seek nicotine. Growers use it as an insecticide in the form of a spray." Available at: https://nyti.ms/47yc0AN (Accessed: August 31, 2025)
75. Raherison, C., Baldi, I., Pouquet, M., et al. (2019) "Pesticides exposure by air in vineyard rural area and respiratory health in children: A pilot study," *Environmental Research*, 169, pp. 189–195. Available at: https://doi.org/10.1016/j.envres.2018.11.002
76. Mayo Clinic (no date) "Nonallergic rhinitis." Available at: https://www.mayoclinic.org/diseases-conditions/nonallergic-rhinitis/symptoms-causes/syc-20351229 (Accessed: August 12, 2024)
77. Dixon, interview
78. ibid.
79. Morrison, interview
80. Thompson, P. (August 14, 2025), interview with A. Ramey
81. Paarlberg, interview
82. Grandjean, P. (2016) "Paracelsus revisited: The dose concept in a complex world," *Basic & Clinical Pharmacology & Toxicology*, 119(2), pp. 126–132. Available at: https://doi.org/10.1111/bcpt.12622
83. Döring, J. (May 21, 2024), email to A. Ramey
84. Vanden Heuvel, J. (May 22, 2025), interview with A. Ramey
85. Hendgen, M., Döring, J., Stöhrer, V., et al. (2020) "Spatial differentiation of physical and chemical soil parameters under integrated, organic, and biodynamic viticulture," *Plants*, 9(10), p. 1. Available at: https://doi.org/10.3390/plants9101361
86. Goode, J. and Harrop, S. (2011) *Authentic Wine: Toward Natural and Sustainable Winemaking*. University of California Press, p. 220
87. Karimi, B., Masson, V., Guilland, C., et al. (2021) "Ecotoxicity of copper input and accumulation for soil biodiversity in vineyards," *Environmental Chemistry Letters*, 19(3), 2013. Available at: https://doi.org/10.1007/s10311-020-01155-x

88. Goldammer, pp. 177–178
89. Zielonka, N. B., Shutt, J. D., Butler, S. J., and Dicks, L. V. (2024) "Management practices, and not surrounding habitats, drive bird and arthropod biodiversity within vineyards," *Agriculture, Ecosystems & Environment*, 367, pp. 10–11. Available at: https://doi.org/10.1016/j.agee.2024.108982
90. Hendgen, et al., p. 3
91. Coll, et al., p. 37
92. Hendgen, et al., p. 8
93. Clark and Tilman, pp. 4–5
94. Lockeretz, p. 63
95. Beaumelle, et al., pp. 5–6
96. Zielonka, et al., p. 2
97. Albrecht, H. and Mattheis, A. (1998) "The effects of organic and integrated farming on rare arable weeds on the Forschungsverbund Agrarökosysteme München (FAM) research station in southern Bavaria," *Biological Conservation* 86(3), pp. 347–356. Available at: https://doi.org/10.1016/S0006-3207(98)00028-7
98. Ritchie, H. (2017) "Is organic really better for the environment than conventional agriculture?," *Our World in Data* [Preprint]. Available at: https://ourworldindata.org/is-organic-agriculture-better-for-the-environment (Accessed: August 12, 2024)
99. Zielonka, et al., p. 1
100. Ostandie, N., Giffard, B., Tolle, P., et al. (2022) "Organic viticulture leads to lower trade-offs between agroecosystem goods but does not improve overall multifunctionality," *Agricultural Systems*, 203, p. 18. Available at: https://doi.org/10.1016/j.agsy.2022.103489
101. Morrison, interview
102. McGourty, interview
103. Seufert, et al., p. 16, citing Allen & Kovach, 2000; Goodman, 2000; Kirchmann & Bergström, 2001; Bahlai, et al., 2010
104. Seufert, et al., pp. 16–17, citing Rosegrant, et al., 2009; Tilman, et al., 2002
105. D'Aversa, R. (April 20, 2024), interview with A. Ramey
106. Sheppard, J. (July 23, 2020) "How do organics and biodynamics affect a vineyard's carbon footprint?," *Decanter*. Available at: https://www.decanter.com/wine-news/vineyard-carbon-footprint-organic-

biodynamic-438356/ (Accessed: August 11, 2024)
107. Jackson, p. 232
108. Goode and Harrop, p. 220
109. Beaumelle, et al., p. 8
110. Döring, et al., p. 235
111. ibid., p. 233
112. Clark and Tilman, pp. 3–5
113. Ritchie
114. Seufert, V., Ramankutty, N., and Foley, J. A. (2012) "Comparing the yields of organic and conventional agriculture," *Nature*, 485, p. 229
115. Brinkley, interview
116. Ostandie, et al., p. 17
117. Döring, et al., p. 237
118. D'Aversa, interview
119. Jones, G. and Grandjean, E. (2017) "Creating the Market for Organic Wine: Sulfites, Certification, and Green Values," Working Paper, Harvard Business School, p. 1. Available at: https://www.hbs.edu/faculty/Pages/item.aspx?num=53619 (Accessed: August 7, 2024)
120. Jeramaz, I. (December 11, 2023), interview with A. Ramey
121. Delmas, M. A., Gergaud, O., and Lim, J. (2016) "Does organic wine taste better? An analysis of experts' ratings," *Journal of Wine Economics*, 11(3), p. 329. Available at: https://doi.org/10.1017/jwe.2016.14
122. Cravero, M.C. (2019) "Organic and biodynamic wines quality and characteristics: A review," *Food Chemistry*, 295, p. 1. Available at: https://doi.org/10.1016/j.foodchem.2019.05.149
123. Mulero, J., Pardo, F., and Zafrilla, P. (2010) "Antioxidant activity and phenolic composition of organic and conventional grapes and wines," *Journal of Food Composition and Analysis*, 23(6), pp. 569–574. Available at: https://doi.org/10.1016/j.jfca.2010.05.001
124. Döring, et al., pp. 235–236
125. Granato, D., de Magalhães Carrapeiro, M., Fogliano, V., and van Ruth, S. M. (2016) "Effects of geographical origin, varietal and farming system on the chemical composition and functional properties of purple grape juices: A review," *Trends in Food Science &*

Technology, 52, pp. 31–48. Available at: https://doi.org/10.1016/j.tifs.2016.03.013

Chapter 4

1. Steiner, R. and Adams, G. (trans) (2012) *Agriculture Course: The Birth of the Biodynamic Method*. Rudolf Steiner Press, p. 53
2. ibid., p. 213
3. Steiner, R. (2007) "Atlantis: The Fate of a Lost Land and Its Secret Knowledge." Rudolf Steiner Press, p. 11
4. Steiner, R. (1912) *The Occult Significance of Blood*. The Colonial Press C. H. Simonds and Co. , p. 31. Available at: https://dn790009.ca.archive.org/0/items/occultsignifican00stei/occultsignifican00stei.pdf
5. Hare, 1922, cited in Paull, J. (2011) "Biodynamic Agriculture: The Journey from Koberwitz to the World, 1924–1938," *Journal of Organic Systems*, 6(1), pp. 212–213. Available at: https://www.researchgate.net/publication/279643274_Biodynamic_Agriculture_The_Journey_from_Koberwitz_to_the_World_1924-1938
6. Steiner (2012), p. 95
7. ibid., pp. 186–192
8. ibid., p. 141
9. ibid., p. 138
10. ibid., p. 272
11. Steiner, R. (June 22, 1924) "To All Members: The Meetings at Koberwitz and Breslau." *Anthroposophical Movement*, p. 10
12. Steiner (2012), p. 290
13. ibid., p. 213
14. Paull, J. (2011) "Biodynamic Agriculture: The Journey from Koberwitz to the World, 1924–1938," *Journal of Organic Systems*, 6(1), p. 32
15. Pfeiffer, E. (2021) *Biodynamic Farming and Gardening: Renewal and Preservation of Soil Fertility* (4th rev. edn). Portal Books: An Imprint of Steiner Books/Anthroposophic Press, p. xii
16. ibid., pp. 133–134
17. ibid., pp. 142–143
18. ibid., pp. 203–204
19. Thun, M. (1999) *Gardening for Life: the Biodynamic Way*. Hawthorn Press, p. 70

20. Truffat, A. (October 23, 2024), interview with A. Ramey
21. Demeter U.S.A. (2023) "Biodynamic Farm Standard, Demeter Association, Inc." Available at: www.demeter-usa.org/downloads/Demeter-Farm-Standard.pdf, p. 6 (Accessed: August 17, 2024)
22. Biodynamic Federation Demeter (2024) "Demeter Wineries Worldwide." Available at: https://demeter.net/wp-content/uploads/2024/04/2024_Demeter-wineries-worldwide.pdf
23. Biodyvin: https://www.biodyvin.com/en/home.html (Accessed: September 13, 2025)
24. Joly, N. (November 20, 2023), interview with A. Ramey
25. ibid.
26. Soto, R. (November 16, 2023), interview with A. Ramey
27. ibid.
28. Camp, C. (August 26, 2024), interview with A. Ramey
29. Reganold, J. P., Palmer, A. S., Lockhart, J. C., and MacGregor, A. N. (1993) "Soil quality and financial performance of biodynamic and conventional farms in New Zealand," *Science*, 260(5106), pp. 344–349. Available at: https://doi.org/10.1126/science.260.5106.344
30. Reganold, J. P. (August 24, 2024), interview with A. Ramey
31. Reeve, J. R., Carpenter-Boggs, L., Reganold, J. P., et al. (2005) "Soil and winegrape quality in biodynamically and organically managed vineyards," *American Journal of Enology and Viticulture*, 56(4), p. 375. Available at: https://doi.org/10.5344/ajev.2005.56.4.367
32. Reganold, interview
33. Döring, J., Collins, C., Frisch, M., and Kauer, R. (2019) "Organic and biodynamic viticulture affect biodiversity and properties of vine and wine: A systematic quantitative review," *American Journal of Enology and Viticulture*, 70, p. 221. Available at: https://doi.org/10.5344/ajev.2019.18047
34. McIntyre, D. (July 5, 2024) "Biodynamic wine has roots in pseudoscience, but the proof is in the bottle," *The Washington Post*. Available at: https://www.washingtonpost.com/food/2024/07/05/biodynamic-farming-wine-rudolph-steiner/ (Accessed: September 13, 2025)
35. Castellini, A., Mauracher, C., and Troiano, S. (2017) "An overview of the biodynamic wine sector," *International Journal of Wine Research*, 9, p. 8. Available at: https://doi.org/10.2147/IJWR.S69126

36. Goode, J. and Harrop, S. (2011), *Authentic Wine: Toward Natural and Sustainable Winemaking*. University of California Press, p. 72
37. Bartlett, M. (September 10, 2024), interview with A. Ramey
38. ibid.
39. Humbrecht, O. (August 24, 2024), interview with A. Ramey
40. Ortiz-Álvarez, R., Ortega-Arranz, H., Ontiveros, V. J., et al. (2021) "Network properties of local fungal communities reveal the anthropogenic disturbance consequences of farming practices in vineyard soils," *mSystems*, 6(3), 10.1128. Available at: https://doi.org/10.1128/msystems.00344-21
41. Belda, I. (October 15, 2024), interview with A. Ramey
42. Kauer, R. (August 28, 2024), interview with A. Ramey
43. Hendgen, M., Hoppe, B., Döring, J., et al. (2018) "Effects of different management regimes on microbial biodiversity in vineyard soils," *Scientific Reports*, 8, 9393. Available at: https://doi.org/10.1038/s41598-018-27743-0
44. Florin, J.-M. (September 5, 2024), interview with A. Ramey
45. Truffat, interview
46. Mayoral, O., Solbes, J., Cantó, J., and Pina, T. (2020) "What has been thought and taught on the lunar influence on plants in agriculture? Perspective from physics and biology," *Agronomy*, 10(7), 955. Available at: https://doi.org/10.3390/agronomy10070955
47. Chalker-Scott, L. (October 4, 2024), interview with A. Ramey
48. Chalker-Scott, L. (October 28, 2024), email to A. Ramey
49. Döring, et al., p. 237
50. Villanueva-Rey, P., Vásquez-Rowe, I., Moreira, M. T., and Feijoo, G. (2014) "Comparative life cycle assessment in the wine sector: Biodynamic vs. conventional viticulture activities in NW Spain," *Journal of Cleaner Production*, 65, p. 330. Available at: https://doi.org/10.1016/j.jclepro.2013.08.026
51. Vásquez-Rowe, I. (October 2, 2024), interview with A. Ramey
52. Villanueva-Rey, et al., p. 332
53. ibid.
54. ibid., pp. 333–334
55. ibid., p. 332
56. Chalker-Scott, interview

57. Steiner, R. (1914, 2019) *An Outline of Occult Science*. Anodos Books, p. 5

Chapter 5

1. Voltaire (1764, 2006) *Voltaire's Philosophical Dictionary*. Project Gutenberg, p. 281
2. Hawkins, E. and Jones, P. D. (2013) "On increasing global temperatures: 75 years after Callendar," *Quarterly Journal of the Royal Meteorological Society*, 139(677), pp. 1961–1963. Available at: https://doi.org/10.1002/qj.2178
3. van Leeuwen, C., Sgubin, G., Bois, B., et al. (2024) "Climate change impacts and adaptations of wine production," *Nature Reviews Earth & Environment*, 5(4), p. 260. Available at: https://doi.org/10.1038/s43017-024-00521-5
4. van Leeuwen, C. (November 29, 2024), interview with A. Ramey
5. ibid.
6. de Rességuier, L., Mary, S., Le Roux, R., et al. (2020) "Temperature variability at local scale in the Bordeaux area. Relations with environmental factors and impact on vine phenology," *Frontiers in Plant Science*, 11. Available at: https://doi.org/10.3389/fpls.2020.00515
7. van Leeuwen, interview
8. ibid.
9. Hannah, L., Roehrdanz, P. R., Ikegami, M., et al. (2013) "Climate change, wine, and conservation," *Proceedings of the National Academy of Sciences of the United States of America*, 110(17), p. 6907. Available at: https://doi.org/10.1073/pnas.1210127110
10. ibid., p. 6910
11. van Leeuwen, C., Schultz, H. R., Garcia de Cortazar-Atauri, I., et al. (2013) "Why climate change will not dramatically decrease viticultural suitability in main wine-producing areas by 2050," *Proceedings of the National Academy of Sciences of the United States of America*, 110(33), pp. E3051–E3052. Available at: https://doi.org/10.1073/pnas.1307927110
12. Gambetta, G. (December 10, 2024), interview with A. Ramey
13. ibid.
14. ibid.

15. van Leeuwen, interview
16. Ladrey, C. (1862) *Revue Viticole: Annales de la Viticulture et de l'Œnologie Françaises et Étrangères*. Librairie de F. Savy, pp. 458–464. Available at: https://gallica.bnf.fr/ark:/12148/bpt6k58127022 (Accessed: September 24, 2025)
17. Adams, L. D. (1973) *The Wines of America*. Houghton Mifflin, p. 162
18. Nemani, R. R., White, M. A., Jones, G. V., et al. (2001) "Asymmetric warming over coastal California and its impact on the premium wine industry," *Climate Research*, 19, p. 31. Available at: https://doi.org/10.3354/cr019025
19. ibid.
20. Smith, S. C. and Alston, J. M. (2024) "Climate, weather, and collective reputation: Implications for California's wine prices and quality," *American Association of Wine Economists*, 11. Available at: https://wine-economics.org/wp-content/uploads/2024/08/AAWE_WP283.pdf
21. Alston, J. (October 25, 2024), interview with A. Ramey
22. Smith, S. (October 25, 2024), interview with A. Ramey
23. Jones, G. (2003) "Climate and terroir: Impacts of climate variability and change on wine," in *Terroir, Geology and Wine: A Tribute to Simon J. Haynes*. The Geological Society of America Annual Meeting, Seattle, Washington, p. 4. Available at: https://www.climateofwine.com/_files/ugd/07f66e_b12281b16d0b45a4a5e1f9943cefb25f.pdf?index=true
24. Alston, interview
25. van Leeuwen, interview
26. Neethling, E. (December 5, 2024), interview with A. Ramey
27. ibid.
28. ibid.
29. ibid.
30. ibid.
31. Bonnardot, V. (November 12, 2024), interview with A. Ramey
32. ibid.
33. ibid.
34. Storchmann, K. (December 4, 2024), interview with A. Ramey
35. ibid.
36. ibid.

Chapter 6

1. Heymann, H. (April 17, 2025), interview with A. Ramey
2. Brillat-Savarin, J. A. and Fisher, M. F. K. (trans) (1995) *The Physiology of Taste, or, Meditations on Transcendental Gastronomy*. Counterpoint Books
3. Francis, L. (April 22, 2025), interview with A. Ramey
4. ibid.
5. Brook, S. (April 22, 2025), interview with A. Ramey
6. ibid.
7. Francis, interview
8. Pearson, W. (April 28, 2025), interview with A. Ramey
9. Heymann, interview
10. Brook, interview
11. Prescott, J. (2012) *Taste Matters: Why We Like the Foods We Do*. London: Reaktion Books
12. Sáenz-Navajas, M.-P., Ballester, J., Pêcher, C., Peyron, D., and Valentin, D. (2013) "Sensory drivers of intrinsic quality of red wines: Effect of culture and level of expertise," *Food Research International*, 54(2), p. 1515. Available at: https://doi.org/10.1016/j.foodres.2013.09.048
13. Pearson, interview
14. Goldstein, R., Almenberg, J., Dreber, A., et al. (2008) "Do more expensive wines taste better? Evidence from a large sample of blind tastings," *Journal of Wine Economics*, 3(1), pp. 1–9
15. Ashton, R. H. (2014) "Wine as an experience good: Price versus enjoyment in blind tastings of expensive and inexpensive wines," *Journal of Wine Economics*, 9(2), pp. 171–182. Available at: https://doi.org/10.1017/jwe.2014.7
16. Goldstein, R. (April 15, 2025), interview with A. Ramey
17. ibid.
18. Brochet, F. (April 25, 2025), interview with A. Ramey
19. ibid.
20. Simons, D. J. and Chabris, C. F. (1999) "Gorillas in our midst: Sustained inattentional blindness for dynamic events," *Perception*, 28, pp. 1059–1074
21. Wang, Q. J. and Prešern, D. (2018) "Does blind tasting work?

Investigating the impact of taining on blind tasting accuracy and wine preference," *Journal of Wine Economics*, 13(4), pp. 384–393. Available at: https://doi.org/10.1017/jwe.2018.36
22. Wang, Q. J. (April 14, 2025), interview with A. Ramey
23. Heymann, interview
24. De Bolla, P. (December 12, 2023), interview with A. Ramey
25. Hodgson, R. T. (2008) "An examination of judge reliability at a major U.S. wine competition," *Journal of Wine Economics*, 3(2), p. 105. Available at: https://doi.org/10.1017/S1931436100001152
26. Brook, interview
27. Grassini, G. (January 16, 2024), interview with A. Ramey

Chapter 7

1. Ariely, D. (December 26, 2023), interview with A. Ramey
2. Anderson, K. (February 26, 2025), interview with A. Ramey
3. ibid.
4. Castriota, S., Corsi, S., Fromento, P., and Ruggeri, G. (2022) "Does quality pay off? 'Superstar' wines and the uncertain price premium across quality grades," *Journal of Wine Economics*, 17(2), p. 151. Available at: https://doi.org/10.1017/jwe.2022.21
5. Corsi, S. (April 29, 2025), interview with A. Ramey
6. Plassmann, H., O'Doherty, J., Shiv B., and Rangel, A. (2008) "Marketing actions can modulate neural representations of experienced pleasantness," *Proceedings of the National Academy of Sciences of the United States of America*, 105(3), pp. 1050–1054. Available at: https://doi.org/10.1073/pnas.0706929105
7. Svitil, K. (January 14, 2008) "Wine study shows price influences perception," *California Institute of Technology News*. Available at: https://www.caltech.edu/about/news/wine-study-shows-price-influences-perception-1374 (Accessed: February 6, 2023)
8. Heymann, H. (April 17, 2025), interview with A. Ramey
9. Kestenbaum, D. and Blumberg, A. (2010) "Episode 189: Why A Dead Shark Costs $12 Million." NPR [Audio Podcast]. Available at: https://www.npr.org/sections/money/2019/03/20/705278696/episode-189-why-a-dead-shark-costs-12-million (Accessed: September 27, 2025)
10. Prisco, J. (August 22, 2022) "The 'world's smallest vineyard' is

selling bottles for $5,000 apiece – but doesn't want you to drink them." CNN. Available at: https://www.cnn.com/style/article/smallest-vineyard-via-mari-10-reggio-emilia/index.html (Accessed: September 27, 2025)
11. Worldwide wealth distribution 2023 (June 16, 2025) Statista. Available at: https://www.statista.com/statistics/203930/global-wealth-distribution-by-net-worth/ (Accessed: February 10, 2023)
12. Ulin, R. (June 9, 2025), interview with A. Ramey
13. ibid.
14. ibid.
15. Laferté, G. (June 11, 2025), interview with A. Ramey
16. ibid.
17. Hobsbawm, E. and Ranger, T. (eds.) (1992) *The Invention of Tradition*. Cambridge: Cambridge University Press (Canto Classics), p. 1. Available at: https://doi.org/10.1017/CBO9781107295636
18. Laferté, interview
19. Demossier, M. (June 4, 2025), interview with A. Ramey
20. ibid.
21. Bourdieu, P. and Nice, R. (trans) (1989) *Distinction: A Social Critique of the Judgement of Taste*. London: Routledge
22. Spence, C. (May 23, 2025), interview with A. Ramey
23. Tal, A., Gvili, Y., and Amar, M. (2022) "To protect and support: Why would consumers find foods tastier if these foods help support a desired self-identity." *Psychology & Marketing*, 39(4), p. 706. Available at: https://doi.org/10.1002/mar.21614
24. Hackel et al. 2018, cited in Tal et al. (2022), p. 705
25. Ariely, interview
26. ibid.
27. Lee, C., Linkenauger, S. A., Bakdash, J. Z., Joy-Gaba, J. A., and Profitt, D. R. (2011) "Putting like a pro: The role of positive contagion in golf performance and perception," *PLOS ONE*, 6(10), p. e26016. Available at: https://doi.org/10.1371/journal.pone.0026016
28. Gomez, P. and Spielmann, N. (2019) "A taste of the elite: The effect of pairing food products with elite groups on taste perceptions," *Journal of Business Research*, 100, pp. 175–183. Available at: https://doi.org/10.1016/j.jbusres.2019.03.013
29. Spielmann, N. (June 13, 2025), interview with A. Ramey

30. Schenk, P. (June 6, 2025), interview with A. Ramey
31. Spielmann, interview
32. Storchmann, K. (December 12, 2024), interview with A. Ramey
33. Spence, interview

Chapter 8

1. Accum, F. C. (1820) *A Treatise on Adulterations of Food, and Culinary Poisons. Exhibiting the Fraudulent Sophistications of Bread, Beer, Wine, Spiritous Liquors, Tea, Coffee, Cream, Confectionery, Vinegar, Mustard, Pepper, Cheese, Olive Oil, Pickles, and Other Articles Employed in Domestic Economy.* Philadelphia: AB'M Small, p. 75. Available at: https://www.gutenberg.org/cache/epub/19031/pg19031-images.html (Accessed: July 20, 2025)
2. Goldberg, K. D. (2011) "Acidity and power: The politics of natural wine in nineteenth-century Germany," *Food and Foodways*, 19(4), p. 300. Available at: https://doi.org/10.1080/07409710.2011.630615
3. ibid., p. 295
4. ibid., p. 305
5. ibid., p. 306
6. Wiley, H.W. (1919) *Beverages and their Adulteration*. P. Blakiston's Son, p. 233
7. ibid., pp. 183–184
8. Pliny the Elder and Rackham, H. (trans.) (1938) *Natural History*. London: W. Heinemann, p. 273. Available at: https://archive.org/details/naturalhistory04plinuoft (Accessed: July 26, 2025)
9. RAW WINE (no date) "Our Charter of Quality." Available at: https://www.rawwine.com/pages/charter-of-quality (Accessed: August 23, 2025)
10. Syndicat de Défense des Vins Nature'l (2022) "Charter of Commitment." Available at: https://vinmethodenature.org/wp-content/uploads/VMN-Charter-of-Committment.pdf
11. Associazione VinNatur (no date) "Procedural Regulations for 'VinNatur Wine' Production." Available at: https://www.vinnatur.org/app/uploads/2024/09/Disciplinare-VinNatur-2020-ENG-1.pdf
12. Mill, J. S. (1874, 1904) "On nature," in *Nature, the Utility of Religion and Theism*. Rationalist Press. Available at: https://www.

lancaster.ac.uk/users/philosophy/texts/mill_on.htm (Accessed: August 18, 2025)
13. Lie, S. A. N. (2016) *Philosophy of Nature: Rethinking Naturalness*. Routledge, pp. 11–18
14. Maule, A. (November 3, 2025), email to A. Ramey
15. Dumont, A. (July 4, 2025), interview with A. Ramey
16. Lie, S. A. N. (July 9, 2025), interview with A. Ramey
17. ibid.
18. Rozin, P. (2005) "The meaning of 'natural': Process more important than content," *Psychological Science*, 16(8), p. 656. Available at: https://doi.org/10.1111/j.1467-9280.2005.01589.x
19. ibid., pp. 656–657
20. Engisch, P. (August 18, 2025), interview with A. Ramey
21. Feiring, A. (July 7, 2025), interview with A. Ramey
22. Dumont, interview
23. Varela, C. (August 19, 2025), interview with A. Ramey
24. RAW WINE, "Our Charter of Quality"
25. Dumont, interview
26. Lapierre, C. (November 21, 2023), interview with A. Ramey
27. Varela, interview
28. Feiring, interview
29. Jefford, A. (August 15, 2025), email to A. Ramey
30. Stockley, C., Paschke-Kratzin, A., Teissedre, P.-L., et al. (2021) SO_2 *and Wine: A Review*. Paris: OIV Publications, p. 5
31. Engisch, interview
32. Syndicat de Défense des Vins Nature'l
33. RAW WINE, "Our Charter of Quality"
34. Stockley, et al., p. 7
35. Brook, S. (April 22, 2025), interview with A. Ramey
36. Zanin, L. (November 6, 2023), interview with A. Ramey
37. Smith, C. (July 25, 2025), interview with A. Ramey
38. Wallard, V. (September 2, 2025), interview with A. Ramey
39. Joly, V. (November 20, 2023), interview with A. Ramey
40. Wallard, interview
41. Heymann, H. (April 17, 2025), interview with A. Ramey
42. Levinovitz, A. (November 10, 2023), interview with A. Ramey
43. ibid.

44. ibid.
45. Meier, B. P., Noreen, E. E., Ji, L.-J., Fellman, M. B., and Lappas, C. M. (2025) "Perceived naturalness biases objective behavior in both tivial and meaningful contexts," *Social Psychological and Personality Science*, 16(1), pp. 105–112. Available at: https://doi.org/10.1177/19485506241276027
46. Meier, B. P. (July 24, 2025), interview with A. Ramey

Index

Accum, Fredrick, 155–6
Addor, Felix, 36
agricultural research, 19th century, 48–50
Alston, Julian, 104–6
American Viticultural Area (AVA), 30–1, 33
Amerine, Maynard, 12
Anderson, Kym, 35, 43, 137
anthropology, and wine appreciation, 143–4
anthroposophism, 84
Appellation d'Origine Controlée (AOC), 7–8, 28–9, 32, 46–7
Ariely, Dan, 148–9
arsenic, used in viticulture, 49, 53, 63
Ashton, Robert, 124
Australian Wine Research Institute (AWRI), 119

Balfour, Lady Eve, 51
Barthes, Roland, 154
Bartlett, Megan, 88
Belda, Ignacio, 89–90
Berrouet, Jean-Claude, 97–8
biodiversity, 69–70, 86
biodynamic vineyards
　arguments for and against, 94–6
　and biodiversity, 86
　Coulée de Serrant vineyard, France, 83–4
　and the environment, 93–4
　and lunar farming, 91–2
　Quintessa Winery, California, 84–5
　skepticism, 92
　and soil, 88–90
　standards and certification, 82–3
　studies on efficacy, 86–8
biodynamic farming, and Rudolf Steiner, 77–80
Biodyvin (European biodynamic certification group), 82–3, 88
biopesticides, 54
BLIC test, 132
blind tasting, 23, 116–17, 124–5, 129, 150
Bois, Benjamin, 21
Bolla, Peter de, 132–3
Bonnardot, Valérie, 111–12
Bordeaux, implications of climate change on winegrowing, 97–8
Bordeaux Mixture, 49–50
Bordeaux Sciences Agro, 98, 101
Bourdieu, Pierre, 146
Brillat-Savarin, Jean Anthelme, 6, 118
Brinkley, Joseph, 73
Brittany, France, replanting of vines, 111–12
Brochet, Frédéric, 125–9, 154
Brook, Stephen, 119, 123, 134, 172
Broude, Tomer, 39–41
Brunier, Daniel, 18
Burgundy, France
　and climate change, 107–8, 110
　grape varieties, 106
　hierarchy of regions, 32
　wine exports to America, 144–5

Cali Natty Wine Fair, California, 157–8
California
   biodynamic vineyards, 84–5
   and climate change, 103–5
   organic farming, 59, 62
   wine judges, 133
   see also Napa Valley
Callendar, Guy Stewart, 98
Camp, Craig, 86
Carson, Rachel, *Silent Spring* (1962), 51, 66–7
Carter, Elizabeth, 42–3
Chalker-Scott, Linda, 92, 95–6
Champagne, 35, 37–8
chaptalization, 173
Château Ausone, 27
Château Cheval Blanc, 26–7
Château d'Yquem, 1811, 141
Château Lafleur, 43
Château Petrus, 97
cheddar cheese, 36
Chile, and water stress, 100
Clarke, Jim, 45
climate, and terroir, 11–13
climate change
   and coastal regions, 111–12
   and economics, 112–13
   and flavour of wine, 97–8
   implications for viticulture, 99–106
   and regional identity, 37–8, 108–10
   responses to, 107–8
   responsibilities of vintners, 113–15
clones, 20
color, influence on taste, 125–9
Confrérie des Chevaliers du Tastevin, 144–5
Corsi, Stefano, 138
Coulée de Serrant vineyard, 83–4, 178

D'Aversa, Ria, 72, 74
DDT (pesticide), 51, 66–7
Demeter (biodynamic certification federation), 80, 81–2, 83, 95

Demossier, Marion, 20–1, 22, 32, 145–6
Denominazione di Origine Controllata e Garantita (DOCG), 8, 44, 47, 135
Dixon, Linley, 64–6
Döring, Dr Johanna, 67, 68
Dornach, Switzerland, Goetheanum (anthroposophical headquarters), 80–1
Douro wine region, demarcation of (1756), 7, 28
drainage, 14, 18
Duchamp, Marcel, 142
Dumont, Ann, 161, 165–6, 167

Engisch, Patrik, 165, 171–2
European Union (EU)
   organic regulations, 53, 59
   protection of geographic names, 35
experimentation, 19th century, 49–50

Fandl, Kevin, 41–2
Feiring, Alice, 165, 169
fining, 20
flaws, in wine, 117–21
Florin, Jean-Michel, 90–1
France
   Appellation d'Origine Controlée (AOC), 7–8, 28–9, 32
   and climate change, 98–9, 107–12
   codification of regions, 32
   National Institute for Origin and Quality (INAO), 97
   National Research Institute for Agriculture, Food and Environment (INRAE), 70
   Saint-Émilion, 26–8
Francis, Leigh, 119, 121, 125
Frank, Albert Bernhard, 57
fungicides, 49

Galloway, B. T., 49
Gambetta, Gregory, 101–2

Geisenheim, University of, winemaking school in, 67, 68, 75, 90
GI (geographic indicator) law, 33–41, 46–7
Goetheanum (anthroposophical headquarters), 80
Goldstein, Robin, 124–5
governments, categorization of vineyards, 32–3
grape bricks, 30
grape varieties
    and climate change, 105–6
    restrictions on, 29, 41–3
Grassini, Graziana, 134–5
Grill Restaurant, New York, 136, 141

Haber, Fritz, 48, 78
Hale, Lauren, 57
Hannah, Lee, 99–101
Hellriegel, Hermann, 57
Heuvel, Justine Vanden, 67–8
Heymann, Hildegarde, 117–18, 123, 131, 139–40, 179
Hirst, Damien, 141–2
Hobsbawm, Eric, *The Invention of Tradition*, 144–5
Hofstetter, Mina, 51
holistic approach, 65–6
homeopathy, 82, 86, 88
Howard, Albert, 50, 61
Howard, Gabrielle, 50
Humbrecht, Olivier, 88–9
Hutchinson, H. B., 50

India, Institute of Plant Industry, 50
Indicazione Geografica Tipica (IGT), 40
irrigation, 18–19, 71, 102–3
    see also water use
Italy
    Denominazione di Origine Controllata e Garantita (DOCG), 8, 44, 47, 135
    and Prosecco, 35–6
    see also Piedmont; Tuscany

Jackson, Ronald, 54–5
Jacquet, Olivier, 22–3, 28, 144
Jeanton, Gabriel, 20
Jefford, Andrew, 170
Jensen, Josh, 11–13
Joly, Nicolas, 83–4
Joly, Valérie, 178
Jones, Greg, 12, 18
Josling, Timothy, 37, 47

Kauer, Randolph, 90
Kimmeridgian soils, 11–12, 112
Könemann, Ewald, 51

Laferté, Gilles, 144–5
Lafon, Dominique, 87
Laforcade, Arnaud de, 27
Lapierre, Camille, 168
Laudan, Rachel, 22
Le Bernadin (restaurant), 118
Leeuwen, Kees van, 10, 98–9, 101, 107
Levinovitz, Alan, 180–1
Liebig, Justus Von, 48–9, 50
Liv-Ex 1000 (database), 150
Lockeretz, William, 61–2
Lodeman, Ernest, 50
lunar farming, 91–2

Madrid Agreement (1891), 29
Maltman, Dr Alex, 8–9
Marketing
    and natural wine, 141–5
    and terroir, 21–3
Masoni, Tullio, 142
Masson, Pierre, 87
Matthews, Dr Mark, 21
Maule, Angiolino, 160–1, 173
McGourty, Glenn, 31, 70–1
mealybugs, 69–70
Medici, Grand Duke Cosimo II, 28
Médoc region, Bordeaux, irrigation, 18
Mega Purple (wine additive), 15, 174
Meier, Brian, 181–2
Mendelson, Richard, 39

Mill, John Stuart, *On Nature*, 159–60, 165
Morris, Jasper, 18
Morrison, Dr Karen, 62, 66, 70
Mosel region, Germany, adulterated wine in, 156
Mursic, Rajko, 25

names, geographic, 33–6
Napa Valley, California, 30–1, 84–5, 105–6
natural wine
   additives and processes, 173–7
   appeal of, 180–2
   definitions, 158–63
   perceptions of, 163–5
   quality of, 178–9
   and sulfur dioxide, 170–3
   and yeast, 165–70
natural wine movement, 157–9
Neethling, Etienne, 108–10
New World wines, use of European names, 34
nitrogen fertilization, 11, 48
Noble, Anne, 117
Noer Lie, Svein Anders, 160, 163
Northbourne, Lord, 51

oak aging, 16
O'Connor, Bernard, 40
organic certification, 52
organic farming
   critiques of, 58–61, 69–72
   origins of, 50–1
   and pesticides, 61–8
   and soil, 56–61, 67–8
Organic Trade Association, 54
organic viticulture
   complexity of, 54–6
   costs, 73–4
   environmental concerns, 68–9
   origins of, 51
   and pesticides, 63–71
   and the soil, 57–61

   yields, 72–3
organic wine
   and consumers, 74–5
   definitions, 52–4

Paarlberg, Robert, 58, 66
Paraclesus (16th century Swiss physician), 67
Paris Convention (1883), 29
Paris wine tasting 1976 ('Judgment of Paris'), 112, 116, 150
Parker, Robert, 105
Pasteur, Louis, 16, 160, 165
Patagonia, winemaking in, 38, 100, 115
Pearson, Wes, 121
pesticides
   development of, 49
   increase in use of in 20th century, 51
   and organic farming, 61–71
Peynaud, Émile, 14, 97
Pfeiffer, Ehrenfried, 81, 86
phylloxera, 22
Piedmont, 40, 107
Pinot Noir, 42
Plassmann, H., 140
Pliny the Elder, on additives in wine, 157
Polyoxin D zinc salt, 54
Portugal, Douro wine region, 7, 28
Prescott, John, 123
prices of wine
   cultural value, 142–51
   and quality, 136–41
Prosecco, controversy over use of name, 35–6
Protected Designation of Origin (PDO), 40, 46

quality, theories of
   blind tastings, 116–17, 124–5
   flawed wine, 117–21
   professional and amateur rankings, 130–5
   see also taste

Rangel, Antonio, 139, 140, 152
RAW WINE (natural wine organization), 158, 166, 168
Real Organic Project, 64
Reganold, John, 56, 86–7
Regenerative Organic Certified (ROC), 95
Rességuier, Laure de, 99
Ribéreau-Gayon, Pascal, 14
Rice, Scott, 54
Richards, E. H., 50
Roberts, Daniel, 15, 17, 19
Rodale, Jerome, 51
rootstock, 19
Rosen, Sherwin, 138
Roupnel, Gaston, 20
Rozin, Paul, 163–4
runoff, agricultural, 60–1

Saint-Émilion, France
    classification system, 26–8
    and climate change, 98
Schenk, Patrick, 153
Seguin, Gerard, 10
sensory science, 117–18, 119
Sideways (film, 2004), 42
Smith, Clark, processes, 176
Smith, Sarah, 104–5
social class, and value of wine, 146–8, 151–2
soil
    and organic farming, 56–61, 67–8
    and terroir, 8–11, 14
Soto, Rodrigo, 84–5
South Africa, low-intervention techniques, 45
Spain, and irrigation, 102
Spence, Charles, 147, 154
Spielmann, Nathalie, 151–2, 153
Spinthiropoulou, Haroula, 56
Sri Lanka, and synthetic fertilizers, 59
Steiner, Rudolf, and origins of biodynamic farming, 77–80, 96
Storchmann, Karl, 112–13, 154

sulfur dioxide, 53, 170–3

Tachis, Giacomo, 135
Tasmania, winemaking in, 38, 100, 115
taste
    and color, 125–9
    cultural influences, 123–4
    experienced and inexperienced drinkers, 124–7
    and genetic differences, 124
    and imperfections, 118–21
    regionally distinctive, 37
    theories of, 122–3, 130–5
tasting panels, 44, 45
terraforming, 17–18
terroir
    and climate, 11–14
    codifying of, 7–8
    and cultural practices, 20–1
    definitions, 15, 21
    first recorded use of word, 7
    and human intervention, 14–19
    and marketing, 21–3
    scientific studies, 23–4
    and soil, 8–11, 14
    and topography, 13
Thompson, Paul, 66
Thun, Maria, 81, 91
tobacco dust, used in viticulture, 63
topography, 11, 13, 17–18
tradition, and value of wine, 144–7
TRIPS agreement (1995), 35
Trubek, Amy, 24, 25
Truffat, Aurélie, 82, 91
Tuscany
    demarcations (1716), 28
    use of Bordelais grapes, 39, 44–5

Ulin, Robert, 143–4
United Kingdom
    increase in vineyards, 101
    winemaking in, 38, 115
United States Department of Agriculture (USDA), organic

regulations, 52–3, 64
United States of America (US)
   American Viticultural Area (AVA), 33
   organic movement, 51–2
   wine production regulations, 29–31, 33
Unwin, Tim, 31

Vannier, Françoise, 9, 10–11
Varela, Cristian, 166, 169
Vásquez-Rowe, Ian, 93–4
vessels, wine, 173
Vin Méthode Nature, 158, 172, 178
VinNatur, 158, 172

Wallard, Vincent, 178–9
Wang, Qian Janice, 130
Ward, Marshall, 50
water use, 43, 71–2, 102–3
   see also irrigation

Whalen, Philip, 20
Wiley, Harvey Washington, 156–7
Wilfahrt, Hermann, 57
Wine and Spirits Education Trust (WSET), 132
Wine Science: Principles and Applications, 54–5
Wine Spectator, 138
Winkler, Albert Julius, 10, 12

yeast assimilable nitrogen (YAN), 11, 169–70
yeasts, 16–17, 165–70

Zanin, Luca, 174–5
Zappalaglio, Andrea, 33, 34–5, 38, 40

Also published by Académie du Vin Library

Académie du Vin Library was founded by Steven Spurrier and friends, dedicated to publishing the finest wine writing, and it has grown into the world's leading wine book publisher in seven short years. We choose our books with care – above all for their readability, but also because we genuinely believe they have something important to say about the world of fine wine that will enhance your drinking pleasure.

The Cynic's Guide to Wine
Sunny Hodge
Sunny Hodge is on a mission to demystify wine. In *The Cynic's Guide to Wine*, he explores the scientific reality behind the drink, from roots in the soil to the flavours we experience when we taste a glass, and shows that the truth is far more fascinating and complex than any wine label could convey.

Behind the Glass: The chemical and sensorial terroir of wine tasting
Gus Zhu MW
What makes red wine red? Do genetic differences, culture and life experience change our perception of wine? And is there science behind the obscure language of tasting notes? The answers to all of these questions and more are explored in *Behind the Glass*, a smart, accessible investigation into the science behind a glass of wine – and our appreciation of it.

Taste the limestone, smell the slate
Alex Maltman

Alex Maltman, emeritus professor of earth sciences at Aberystwyth University, finds himself between a rock and a vineyard place as he explains how a wine's flavours relate to the geology at foot, and discovers that there is more to 'minerality' than mud, rocks and the earth's stark materials

Rooted in Change: The Stories Behind Sustainable Wine
Jane Masters MW and Andrew Neather

Jane Masters, a Master of Wine with a profound commitment to sustainability in the global wine industry, and Andrew Neather, a respected journalist and former wine critic for the *London Evening Standard* provide a thoughtful and accessible exploration of how the wine industry can evolve in response to the greatest challenges of our era.

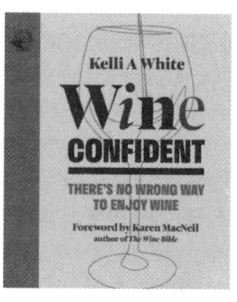

Wine Confident: There's No Wrong Way to Enjoy Wine
Kelli A White

Kelli White loves every aspect of wine and wants to ignite the same kind of passion in her readers. For those who have fallen in love with wine already, this book is an imaginative and practical guide to embarking on its greatest adventures. For those who haven't yet, it is the spark to light the fuse.

Browse the full list and buy online at academieduvinlibrary.com